INTERCULTURAL UNDERSTANDING

Fall 2007

Number 2 in a Series of Monographs Addressing Critical Issues in the Education of English Language Learners

Funded in part by the Federation of North Texas Area Universities

A project of the Bilingual/ESL Committee of the Federation of North Texas Area Universities

Phap Dam, Ph.D.
Texas Woman's University
Series Editor

Melinda T. Cowart, Ed.D.
Texas Woman's University
Managing Editor

INTERCULTURAL UNDERSTANDING
Fall 2007

Phap Dam, Ph.D., Texas Woman's University
Series Editor

Melinda T. Cowart, Ed.D., Texas Woman's University
Managing Editor

ISBN 0-9772129-8-X

Cover design by CANH NAM
Photo credits: Dao Thi Hoi, Ed.D.
American Teacher (an AFT publication)

Book design and Desktop publishing by VICANA

Copyright © 2007 by the Federation of North Texas Area Universities.

All rights reserved. No part of this publication may be reproduced in any form or by any electronic or mechanical means including information storage and retrieval system, except for educational purposes.

Printed by
May King Enterprise, Co. Ltd.
Under the imprint of CANH NAM Publishers, Inc.

Introduction

The real world of school in the United States is one of much cultural, linguistic, and academic diversity where students of numerous cultural and language groups believe that the educators who teach them will possess adequate knowledge about their experiences, beliefs, values and educational needs to facilitate educational success. While the teaching force in the United States continues to reflect little diversity, it has been estimated that 70% of teachers who work with the linguistically diverse student population have had no training in bilingual or ESL education. It is significant that newcomers as well as culturally diverse students who were born in the United States and teachers may have quite different notions regarding what should occur at school and in the classroom. In order to compensate for the mismatch of a diverse student population and a teacher corps that lacks diversity, it is imperative that appropriate and effective teacher preparation and development be provided.

The knowledgeable and caring educator of diverse populations embarks on a journey of discovery about self and others, developing a sense of intercultural understanding that guides perception and critical educational decisions. Intercultural understanding implies an understanding of language and how it is used in relationships. It includes an understanding of the dynamic nature of culture in general and the knowledge that there is difference and variety within and among various cultural groups. Intercultural understanding entails a willingness to be a student of diverse cultures and their component languages, behaviors, values, and beliefs. When students perceive that a teacher has chosen to learn about their unique life experiences, they sense that they are welcome in the classroom. Similarly, students who see themselves reflected in the school curriculum tend to believe that school is a place for them. The expectation is that as intercultural understanding increases, academic achievement is enhanced.

Therefore, the Bilingual/ESL Committee of the Federation of North Texas Area Universities presents a monograph entitled ***Intercultural Understanding***. Second in a series of monographs addressing critical issues in the education of English language learners, the monograph represents a compendium of information, current trends, and research associated with exploring and promoting intercultural understanding. In addition, a discussion of the impact of intercultural sensitivity and understanding in bilingual and ESL classrooms is incorporated. Because the anticipated audience for the monograph includes preservice and inservice teachers and administrators as well as university faculty and students, every effort has been made to present articles that address topics and themes that are essential to the effective equitable teaching of all students. Two articles explore issues pertaining to acculturation. Dr. Cowart looks at the loss and hope associated with the refugee experience and the acculturation process and indicates how teachers may ease the transition for refugee students as they search for a dual identity. Drs. Anderson and Carver-Cyr investigate the perspectives of adolescents regarding culture, diversity, and intercultural interactions. Three articles look at different issues related to language difference and intercultural understanding. Dr. Dam addresses and explains some common predictable errors Spanish-speaking children tend to make as they learn English. Dr. Chou investigates certain factors affecting the acquisition of English for English language learners (ELLs) with implications for Intensive English Language Institutes in the United States. Dr. Kinnison, Dr. Stephens, Mr. Stager, and Ms. Rueter use their expertise in the field of special education to look into the appropriate use of scores on tests of Cognitive Academic Language Proficiency (CALP) for educational decision-making for ELLs. Creating or establishing a community is the theme of two articles. Dr. Mathis discusses the use of multicultural children's literature and text sets to assist teachers and students in developing a sense of community, and incorporates lists of books and possible text sets to use in the classroom. Drs. Rademacher, Dunlap, and Pemberton provide numerous suggestions for establishing a positive environment in the classroom utilizing lessons that can be gleaned from the flight habits of geese.

Three articles explore important matters related to teacher education and development. Drs. Wilhelm, Cowart, and Rademacher share the results of several years of using a fear reduction activity known as the community plunge to assist preservice teachers in putting aside their concerns regarding teaching diverse student populations in a location that has a poor media reputation. Lessons learned and comments from former participants are included. Drs. Repman, Chance, Kenney, and Parsons tell of a very interesting and unique partnership they have developed with some schools in the United Kingdom for the purpose of enhancing new teachers' preparedness for teaching in diverse settings. Drs. Casey and Abrego consider the types of needs preservice bilingual teachers who are enrolled in alternative certification programs may have and how districts may retain these new teachers by attending to some of the more pressing needs.

Parental involvement is the topic of two of the articles. While Dr. Robles-Goodwin discusses several practices that have proven to be successful in involving Latino parents in particular, Drs. Salazar and Garza explore how to establish positive home-school connections with ethnically diverse parents.

Finally, Drs. Rodriguez, Cowart, and Dam provide a glossary of key terms and concepts related to the theme of the monograph, intercultural understanding. Several updated sources of information associated with the terms and concepts are included.

By creating this monograph regarding the development and enhancement of intercultural understanding, the Bilingual/ESL Committee seeks to provide current and accurate information that will assist teachers, administrators, and teacher educators in understanding their students, the parents of their students, and best practices for addressing their unique needs. The information and strategies that are discussed in this monograph are intended for practical use by practitioners at every level. Thus, the language is intended to be scholarly, yet not intimidating.

Dr. Dam and Dr. Cowart, editors of the monograph, wish to thank the Federation of North Texas Area Universities and the Texas Woman's University College of Professional Education for their significant and extensive support of this project. Their considerable generosity enables the Bilingual/ESL Committee of the Federation to provide this second monograph in the series at no cost to educators and students.

The current monograph is second in a series of monographs that address the challenges and issues inherent in learning and teaching English as a second language. The first monograph, *Cultural and Linguistic Issues for English Language Learners,* was published in 2006. The Call for Manuscripts for the third monograph appears at the end of this publication. The editors remain dedicated to the continuation of this challenging and rewarding endeavor.

TABLE OF CONTENTS

Loss and Hope: Challenges in Acculturation for Refugee Children in the United States	Melinda T. Cowart	1
Echoes of Diversity: Adolescent Voices and Perspectives	Gina B. Anderson Elizabeth Carver-Cyr	21
Mother-Tongue Interference in Spanish-Speaking English Language Learners' Interlanguage	Phap Dam	44
Factors Affecting English Language Learners' Acquisition of English: Implications for English Language Institutes	Emily Chou	58
Using Cognitive Academic Language Proficiency (CALP) Scores to Enhance Educational Decision-Making for Students from Language Minority Backgrounds	Lloyd Kinnison Tammy L. Stephens Phillip Stager Jessica A. Rueter	74
Contemplating Community through Multicultural Children's Literature	Janelle Mathis	92
Creating an Inclusive Learning Community: Lessons from the Geese	Joyce Rademacher Karen Dunlap Jane Pemberton	114
The Community Plunge: A Cultural Immersion Experience for Preservice Teachers	Ron Wilhelm Melinda T. Cowart Joyce Rademacher	133
Collaboration to Foster Intercultural Understanding: The International Learning Community Model	Judy Repman Cindi Chance Stephanie Kenney	162

Influence of Background Experiences on the Support Needs of Alternatively Certified Novice Bilingual Teachers	Patricia Casey Michelle Abrego	177
Braiding Cultural Understandings: Reflections of a Teacher Working with Diverse Latino Parents	Patsy J. Robles-Goodwin	200
Supporting Positive Home-School Connections with Ethnic Minority Parents	Dora L. Salazar Mary F. B. Garza	232
Glossary of Key Terms and Concepts in Intercultural Understanding	Rudy Rodriguez Melinda T. Cowart Phap Dam	241

CALL FOR MANUSCRIPTS 259

AUTHORS' INFORMATION 263

Loss and Hope: Challenges in Acculturation for Refugee Children in the United States

Melinda T. Cowart
Texas Woman's University

> You never know what's going to happen next. Like my family before – they rich. They have a good house, a good family. They have good everything in my country. But what come next? Just like a minute, and it's gone. Everything is gone. My dad used to be a soldier. He got a car, a motorcycle, a house – everything better than right now. The Khmer Rouge come and it's gone. Now we poor like, you know, really poor.
> --Dong Hua, Refugee student and member of the Blue Dragon Explorer Post

Dong was the member of our youth group who protested the most when asked to record on a video camera his experiences as a refugee in America. The Blue Dragon Explorer Post was created in the early 1980's by the author and her husband, a Dallas police officer at the time. The post consisted initially of refugee youth who had recently been resettled in America. Later the group grew to include first and second generation Asian immigrants as well as youth from several different cultural groups. Members of the Blue Dragon Explorer Post had approached KERA, the local affiliate for PBS television, about the possibility of creating a documentary about their experiences growing up in the United States. The goal of the documentary was to honestly depict the challenges that are inherent to growing up and developing a bicultural identity as refugees or immigrants in the U.S. with the hope that their teachers and peers might have a better understanding of what they had

INTERCULTURAL UNDERSTANDING

experienced. An executive producer adopted the project and worked to ensure that the integrity of the documentary was maintained by insisting that the youth of the Blue Dragons tell their stories in their own words, addressing what they perceived to be their biggest issues. The members were responsible for identifying and filming important stories, selecting the stories through the editing process, writing the narrative, and narrating the final product. Group members were asked to take home high 8 cameras for days and weeks at a time in order to capture on film aspects of their lives that would best give a picture of the challenges of adapting to U.S. American society as well as their hopes, worries, conflicts and dreams. With enthusiasm and sometimes startling honesty, several members immediately set out to tell their stories as newcomer immigrants and refugees in America. Topics such as cultural differences in the respect and treatment afforded to elders, relationships with mothers, relationships with fathers, discrimination at school and in society, the difficulties of learning English, different treatment for girls and boys in the native cultures, concerns about parents, concerns about loved ones left in the home country, and the clash of home and school culture were addressed. The result was a documentary, *Through the Eye of the Dragon*, which aired in 1998 and poignantly portrayed from the perspective of adolescent and young adult refugees and immigrants what is essentially involved in balancing two cultures and two languages when attempting to acculturate in America.

Yet, when Dong was approached for the filming of his unique story, he responded by saying he had nothing to tell, that there was nothing inside of him to share. After much cajoling, my husband, the project manager and I were able to get Dong to agree to a brief Saturday morning filming/interview session in which I would ask him a series of questions about his experiences in his homeland, during escape as a refugee, in the refugee camp, and in the new host country, the U.S. It was a beautiful fall morning when we met in a city park near Dong's home to conduct the interview. When the questioning commenced, the young man who had declared that he had nothing to share, nothing to say, nothing inside, poured out his heart for over two hours. The dam of quiet solitude seemed to break as the horrors he had previously experienced in Cambodia and during flight to a place of safety, the disappointments, fears and hopes about life in America, worries about his mom and sister left behind, and concerns about his clinically depressed father with whom he lived overflowed.

It was during this experience that I realized that even after two decades of working with refugee and other newcomer youth both at school and in after school activities, there was much to learn regarding the emotions, feelings, worries, fears, hopes and desires that make up the affective aspect of acculturation for each individual student. It occurred to me once again that there are two paths to the same goal of success for all children. One path is fraught with frustration, anxiety, and failure. The other still includes challenges, but without needless barriers strewn along the way by those who lack the intercultural understanding to accurately interpret behavior, assess, diagnose, and effectively and equitably teach the newest student populations. Unfortunately, teachers sometimes unknowingly set up cultural borders for refugee, immigrant, and political asylum students by not recognizing their unique experiences of flight and survival as well as their concerns and motivations (Gollnick & Chinn, 2006). Such students already face a lifetime of negotiating a bicultural existence. A knowledgeable educator may assist students in achieving, excelling, learning, and having the opportunity to be all that they may be by refraining from erecting cultural barriers.

A significant component of intercultural understanding for teachers is possessing enough knowledge about students and their distinctive experiences to be able to comprehend them culturally as though looking through an emic, or in-group, lens even though the educator may actually be etic, or outside of the students' various cultural groups. The purpose of this article is two-fold – to explore some of the school and home challenges that many refugee students encounter as they create a new life in the United States, and to assist educators in augmenting their intercultural knowledge and understanding for refugee students and their families.

The refugee experience

It is essential to note that refugee children such as Dong and other members of the Blue Dragons frequently must endure a degree of social, emotional, mental and physical upheaval that is more intense than any event most adults in the United States might imagine. Defining a refugee as someone who has fled across an international border in order to seek safe haven, the United Nations High Commissioner for Refugees (UNHCR) further states that a refugee is a person outside of the United States who seeks protection on the grounds that to remain in the homeland would mean persecution or death because of race, religion, membership in a social group, political opinion or national origin (World Refugee Survey, 2005). As conditions deteriorate in the home country refugee children and their families may experience deprivation, hunger, ethnic cleansing, civil war, loss of loved ones, and even torture. As a survivor of the Cambodian Holocaust Loung Ung (2000) describes what her sister, Keav, suffered as she grew increasingly ill from starvation and dysentery that went untreated:

> An hour after she leaves the field, Keav finally arrives at the makeshift hospital where there are many patients waiting to see the nurses. The hospital is a decrepit old building with many cots lined up on the ground. When Keav approaches a nurse and reports her illness, the nurse takes her arm and leads her to a cot to lie down. Without taking her pulse or touching her, the nurse asks Keav a few brief questions about her symptoms and hurries away, saying she will return later to check on her and bring her some medicine. Keav knows this is a lie. There is no medicine. There are no real doctors or nurses, only ordinary people ordered to pretend to be medical experts. All the real doctors and nurses were killed by the Angkar long ago. (p. 96)

Hours later fifteen year old Keav died before her parents could reach her.

Some children have had the misfortune of being conscripted as soldiers by warring factions in their home countries and have been forced to commit atrocities in order to survive. While most people would consider the notion that children would be used as instruments of war to be abhorrent, unthinkable, children all too often represent a never-ending source of fresh recruits in countries experiencing widespread genocide or ethnic cleansing. Some refugee children arrive in the United States as unaccompanied minors, having lost their parents and siblings to the wars in which they were forced to fight. A former child soldier in Sierra Leone, Ishmael Beal (2007) recounts one of many occasions in which he was ordered as a young boy to shoot and kill:

> My face, my hands, my shirt and gun were covered with blood. I raised my gun and pulled the trigger, and I killed a man. Suddenly as if someone was shooting them inside my

brain, all the massacres I had seen since the day I was touched by war began flashing in my head. Every time I stopped shooting to change magazines and saw my two young lifeless friends, I angrily pointed my gun into the swamp and killed more people. (p. 119)

Whatever series of events or conditions precipitates the need to leave, the escape is almost always characterized by panic and terror. After the decision to flee has been made, the refugees must escape through a gauntlet of enemy soldiers and landmines to get to a place of general safety (Warwick, Neville, & Smith, 2006). Typically a refugee camp has been established in a country of first asylum by the UNHCR. The refugee camp becomes home to the new refugees yet without the familiarity of the language, culture, traditions, values and beliefs of the home that was left behind. For the refugee family any hope of organized, legal resettlement in the United States rests with being officially processed while still in the refugee camp by a refugee resettlement agency under the authority of the U.S. State Department (U.S. Committee for Refugees and Immigrants, 2006). While the resettlement process is complex and may be quite lengthy, most refugees recognize that enduring and completing the process provides a glimmer of hope for the improved existence that was anticipated when they fled.

Refugee resettlement in the United States

In 2005 there were 12 million displaced persons in the world with 176,700 who were officially designated as refugees and asylum seekers calling the United States home for the first time. The total number of refugees resettled in the U.S. for that year alone was 53,725. They arrived from many countries, including Somalia, Iran, Burma, Sudan, Ethiopia, and Vietnam. Florida,

INTERCULTURAL UNDERSTANDING

Minnesota, Texas, California, and Washington were the five states that received the largest numbers of new arrivals (World Refugee Survey, 2006).

Many of the newcomers were school-aged children who entered U.S. public schools for the first time. Included in that group were children who arrived with one parent, two parents, or as unaccompanied minors with no parents. The most fortunate new students were those who encountered teachers who were either willing to increase their knowledge of the refugee experience or educators who were already well informed and were able to ease the transition of the uprooted. Warwick, Neville, and Smith (2006) state that daily commonplace experiences serve to either help or harm the adjustment of refugee children. The newcomer students commonly suffer further poverty, exclusion, anxiety, and insecurity upon resettlement in the new host country. They arrive at school with emotional states that may be in upheaval or turmoil because of what has already occurred in their lives. Ung (2006) recalls a sense of isolation due to the lack of information many Americans exhibit regarding the refuge experience:

> I'm lying on my side on the floor, when the trailer for *The Killing Fields* splashes across our TV screen. The commercial begins with a group of helicopters flying into view like a swarm of dragonflies, then cuts to scenes of bombs dropping into Cambodia and the Khmer Rouge soldiers storming into Phnom Penh.
>
> From somewhere inside my brain the smell of putrid flesh leaps off the television and fills my nostril. I blink but the smell remains and attacks my eyes, making them water. My scalp starts to sweat while my heart squeezes into a tight fist. Lightly, I scratch my feet and crack my toes to distract myself from the smell.

"Americans will never know what it was truly like," I think. (p. 124)

Stress factors during acculturation

Experts in the field of second language acquisition in their discussion of the role of the affective filter speak to the power of the unsettled emotional state to filter or block learning (Dulay, Burt, & Krashen, 1982). In fact, a high affective filter, whereby a student feels anxious, upset, worried, or concerned about prior events or threatened in the current situation basically ensures that little learning will take place. What in addition to the culture shock of attending school in a new country and learning in an unfamiliar language might create a disequilibrium of a refugee child's emotional state? Dong, in his interview, and the other Blue Dragons in their documentary enumerated multiple issues that cause such discomfort that they might be unable to focus on the learning that was to take place. Three of the more frequently stated issues include

- parents who struggle to adjust and may be unable to parent,
- concerns about parents and siblings left in the home countries, and
- cultural bereavement and cultural conflict.

<u>Refugee parents who struggle to adjust</u>

Many refugee children suffer from depression because of the violence and trauma they have experienced (Pang, 2005). Acculturative stress among these children stems from numerous sources, including the challenges of developing a dual cultural identity while receiving inadequate guidance and supervision from parents who are too traumatized to parent (Aronowitz, 1984).

Their parents, having endured the same violence, loss, and horrors may also experience periods of depression and even the more severe post traumatic stress disorder (PTSD). Among child and adult refugees from war zones the incidence of PTSD is estimated to be somewhere between a low of 25% and a high of 94%. Several factors, including the severity and prevalence of the traumatic events, general attentiveness to preparing for the catastrophic upheaval, and the existence or absence of spirituality determine the severity of PTSD among refugee adults (Kemp & Rasbridge, 2004). Symptoms of PTSD consist of, among others, nightmares, flashbacks of traumatic experiences, depression, and fear that the same events may be happening again.

It is essential to note that the first few months after resettlement may not be the most difficult time emotionally and may not be marked by any overt symptoms of PTSD. This is a period characterized by almost euphoric happiness over having made it to a place of safety. It is generally during the second year of resettlement, a time associated with extreme culture shock, that the symptoms of PTSD build and reach their peak (Portes & Rumbaut, 2006). Therefore, refugee parents and their children arrive in the U.S. and experience a two-year cycle in which they are at first ecstatic to be alive only to descend into depression by the second year, despairing of the very life the escape was intended to preserve. Simultaneously an intense period of adjustment to a new culture, language, value, and belief system must occur. For some refugee parents the changes are simply overwhelming, and they find it too difficult to take care of themselves and their families while providing adequate emotional guidance and support for their children.

During the interview with Dong, the reluctant informant, it became apparent that his father exhibited symptoms of depression and possibly PTSD. Describing him as sleeping all of the time and never wanting to go outside of their apartment, Dong and his brothers sensed that something was not right with their father. Dong explained what his father meant when he said that he felt like he was in jail:

> What my dad needs is love and friends. Over here you go to work, come home and sleep. You don't even know what happens. People live and die and you don't even care when they fall down. That's American people. In Cambodia we always have each other. We always invite each other to visit each other's families and eat and talk. We love each other in the neighborhood. But over here, it's go to work and come home. What you care for is your family. You don't care about other people. My dad, he don't have nobody to care for him. And he have no love. That's why he feels like he in jail. Just like in jail there is no love, no care, no nothing.
> --Dong, refugee student and Blue Dragon member

Because Dong's mother had been left behind in Cambodia, his father had no one in his life to provide the support he needed. Further questioning revealed that his father did not seek assistance for any of his problems. Instead he believed that as a Cambodian man and a Buddhist he should be self-sufficient, refraining from complaining. Like other refugee men who become vulnerable during the refugee experience, his father may have perceived a threat to his former social identity (Eisenbruch, de Jong, & van de Put, 2004). Also, he reasoned that he should not appear to be begging for help in America. Thus, his condition did not rapidly improve.

Portes and Rumbaut (2006) note that lengthy journeys such as those inherent to refugee resettlement usually include overwhelming life events such as loss, change, stressful demands and conflict that present a strong challenge to the emotional stability of the newcomers. Similarly, Igoa (1995) observed that parents may suffer homesickness, sadness, anxiety about the future, and frustration during first efforts at establishing themselves in their new host country. As in Dong's case, children are quick to detect the angst and worries of their parents. When their parents are unable to provide the comfort, security, and stability associated with parenting, the children may have feelings of helplessness (Igoa, 1996). The loss of parental support, even if for only a brief period, may force the children of refugees to take on adult responsibilities, such as paying the bills, translating for doctors, and dealing with a landlord, in order to assist their families during a time of great transition (Cowart, 2006). The well-being of parents has been found to be a type of protective element on the mental health of refugee children. In addition, parental involvement in school for refugee children has been identified as a factor that positively affects school and social adjustment (Delgad-Gaitan, 1991). When a parent is unable to be involved in school or lacks the well-being to guide and direct a child's acculturation experience, a concerned teacher may play a supportive role in the adjustment of a refugee child by providing a listening ear, refraining from making erroneous assumptions regarding the failure of the parent to participate in school functions, providing culturally relevant instruction, using the child's heritage language as a valuable resource for teaching English as a second language, and providing guidance in developing a bicultural identity (Igoa, 1995; Nieto, 2008). Igoa (1995) suggests that when an educator comprehends the fundamental causes of a refugee student's often overwhelming emotions, he or she will more effectively identify the type of support the child may need.

INTERCULTURAL UNDERSTANDING

<u>Concerns about parents and siblings left in the home country</u>

Sometimes during the rush to escape to a safe haven, family members get left behind. They may have been separated during a mass exodus such as what occurred in Cambodia, Kosovo, and the Sudan. Loved ones may have delayed their travels and waited in the home country so that additional family members might accompany them. In the case of Dong's mother and sister, they were left behind because Dong's father feared for their safety en route. He believed they were safer waiting for him to send for them after he reached a safe place in a stable environment. Thus, began the agony of separation from beloved family members which has existed for this family for more than two decades.

When refugee parents and other relatives are left behind, it is difficult, if not impossible for them to provide comfort for the children who have been resettled in another country as refugees. Additionally, there are few opportunities to correspond with anyone who remained in the home country (National Center for Child Traumatic Stress). Loung Ung (2005) had already experienced the death of both of her parents and several other family members while she lived as a small child under the regime of Pol Pot. When her older brother arranged for an escape, he was only able to take three people, including himself. He selected his fiancée and Loung, his ten-year-old sister, leaving an eleven-year-old sister and some brothers behind in Cambodia, not knowing if or when they would be able to communicate once they were resettled. Loung alludes to her sense of loss as she grew up in America with so many family members and memories far away:

> In the dark I lay my head on its cushioned armrest and lie diagonally across the rocking chair. Outside the window, above the phone and power lines, the moon frowns and the stars twinkle like the lights on the pine tree. As the chair

rocks back and forth, I bring my legs to my chest and curl into a fetal position. "It's Christmas," I say to myself. "You should be happy. Everybody's happy on Christmas." The sobs come faster now, pushing against my diaphragm and out of my throat. "But I am so lonely." I cover my hand over my mouth so Meng and Eang won't hear me. I don't want them to know. "I miss my sisters," I say aloud to an empty room… When the other kids brag about what their parents bought them for Christmas, I am silent because I want nothing from Ma and Pa. I just want them to be here. I want to sit on Pa's lap. I want to see Ma's smile. I just want them to be alive. (p. 94)

During the interview in which Dong released so many of the emotions that had built up inside of him since his refugee experience began, he described his sadness over leaving his mother and sister behind in Cambodia. He stated that sometimes after going out with friends and enjoying himself, he felt intense guilt because he knew that his mother was living such a difficult life in the home country. Dong went on to say that sometimes he didn't want to live any more because of his mother's and sister's predicament. Almost in the same breath Dong expressed a bit of anger towards his father for asking him for money to send to his mother and for not taking better care of him.

Unfortunately, refugee parents who accompanied children seldom have the time to devote to establishing the routines and stability that would serve to comfort the child who is concerned about those left back home. Consequently, when signs of distress, culture shock, and depression present themselves in refugee children, the symptoms may be overlooked or misunderstood (National Center for Child Traumatic Stress, 2003). Many refugee children show evidence of trauma, but few receive care (Rousseau,

INTERCULTURAL UNDERSTANDING

1995). In cases such as these there is the possibility that refugee children may begin to have a concern about issues of adjustment in the United States, including loss, what their new lives may be like, and what persons they may trust to guide them. Eisenbruch (1988) termed these trepidations and anxieties cultural bereavement.

Cultural bereavement

Cultural bereavement is the sense of being separated from the past and losing touch with all that is familiar from the homeland. Survivor's guilt, anger, and ambivalence or feeling multiple emotions at one time, characterize the sentiments associated with cultural bereavement among children (Eisenbruch, 1988). When refugee children and adolescents make strides in learning English, learning in school, and adapting to U. S. American culture and society, every step forward may symbolize a further departure from what was comfortable, memorable, meaningful, and recognizable in the homeland. As a result, their sense of loss and cultural bereavement may be exacerbated by successful steps toward acculturation. Without a caring and knowledgeable adult to guide the acculturation experience and to provide reassurance that learning a new language and culture does not mean that the heritage language and culture must be eliminated or forgotten, the refugee student will flounder, literally taking one step forward and two steps back out of fear of losing his or her cultural identity. For example, Dong shared that he wanted to stay out of trouble so he started attending a Presbyterian church and participating with their youth group. Feeling good about his positive steps forward, he informed his Cambodian friends and invited them to join him. His friends responded with criticism, asking if he was trying to forget his Cambodian Buddhist heritage.

Dong decided not to return in order to avoid the in-group conflict associated with the appearance of giving up or losing his culture.

Another aspect of cultural bereavement is the result of the acculturation process whereby refugee children and adolescents spend their school days trying to learn how to act like American children only to go home and frighten their families over what appears to be an abandonment of the home culture. Loung Ung (2005) notes:

> Sometimes I want to scream at Eang and her many rules. After 3 years in America, she is still trying to raise me to be a proper Cambodian. And it seems that in addition to not swearing, a proper Cambodian girl doesn't go out to movies with male friends, go to the mall, listen to loud music, talk for more than 5 minutes on the phone, come home after dark, or go anywhere by herself. It seems to me a proper Cambodian girl is just supposed to sit at home and be quiet. But I am no proper Cambodian girl. And in English the bad words blow off of my lips without much shame or fear, yet I can't even silently mouth these same swear words in Chinese or Khmer without feeling like a very bad girl. (p. 100)

Refugee children commonly feel torn between the heritage culture and language of the homeland and the culture and language of the new country (National Center for Child Traumatic Stress, 2003). The acculturation process includes long periods of trying out newly learned words, gestures, and behaviors. Much of this is transient in nature. It is noteworthy that as the newcomers learn a new language and a new set of cultural practices, they will still not associate strong emotions with the new structures. Accordingly, English language learners (ELLs) may use what is considered to be taboo language when trying to communicate in a manner that is acceptable to peers only to find out that the words convey something rude or vulgar in the first language. The school setting may serve to place additional stress on the refugee child or adolescent through its cultural misunderstanding of the children's behaviors. The informed educator will interpret these seemingly rude behaviors as stages of adjustment during the acculturation process and aid the newcomer ELL in learning what is acceptable.

Igoa (1995) states that acculturation is a process of adaptation that permits individuals to participate in a new mainstream culture in a new place without having to give up their own heritage culture. Acculturation has been shown to serve as a protective factor in helping refugee children and adolescents cope with the stress of refugee resettlement. Similarly, it can ease the great transition that will surely be necessary as they adapt to the new host country (National Center for Child Traumatic Stress, 2003). It would appear that the only appropriate course of action for teachers working with refugee and immigrant populations would be to promote a positive acculturation experience. The issues that have been discussed in this article have nothing to do with pedagogy. Rather they pertain to affairs of the heart. They do not have to be barriers to learning a new language or content. How may a teacher who is aware that some of her students might be concerned about parents who are too traumatized to parent, or may have worries about parents who have been left behind in the home country, or that there are students who are experiencing cultural bereavement assist those students so that acculturation is the adaptation process of choice? What can an educator do to promote successful positive acculturation? Selected recommendations follow:

- Investigate to find out why a parent might not be involved in school functions. Rarely is the reason a parent's lack of concern.

INTERCULTURAL UNDERSTANDING

- Search for subtle ways to help the parent feel more comfortable discussing school topics with you.
- Identify what the parent's expectations of schools and teachers were in the home country.
- Note that no matter how difficult life may have been in the home country, the refugee student will most likely miss home and all that it represents, including cultural familiarity, loved ones, friends, and memories of a happier time.
- Refrain from blaming or criticizing the parent who may be temporarily unable to parent. Provide opportunities for the refugee child in these circumstances to feel good enough about the situation to be able to carry on with learning and the acculturation process.
- Give students a voice, an outlet for telling their stories. Art projects, interviews, journals, storytelling, and music are among several ways for involving students in a meaningful manner in their own adjustment.
- Realize that refugee children and adolescents may be especially vulnerable to emotional upset because they are at a developmental stage where they are establishing their identity as individuals at the same time that the refugee experience is forcing them to create a dual identity in a new country.
- Become or continue to be a student of cultures and languages, particularly those of your students so that your knowledge of their experiences and needs will grow regularly.

INTERCULTURAL UNDERSTANDING

- Use culturally relevant materials and books in the classroom so that your students may see themselves and others reflected in the curriculum.
- Be the caring, informed adult who can, for a brief period of time, help the child to find his or her own way to a bicultural and bilingual identity.

Conclusion

Much remains to be learned about all that refugee children, adolescents, and parents must endure as they bravely seek a new life in a new land. Their journey lasts for their entire lives. The children of refugees in the United States are entrusted to the teachers in U.S. public schools with the hope that they will learn English and become contributing members of American society without having to abandon all that was once so dear in their heritage cultures. The resettlement of refugees will continue in the United States because of the principles of freedom by which the country was founded. Educators can powerfully support their newcomer students by being familiar with their needs and previous lives and cultures, selecting appropriate strategies, using culturally relevant curricula, and by avoiding stereotypical thinking. The strongest welcome that an educator can be provided is the gift of accurate information coupled with time, patience, and confidence in the abilities of newly arriving refugee students and their families to successfully adjust to the new lives of freedom and safety they wished to pursue.

References

Aronowitz, M. (1984). The social and emotional adjustment of immigrant children: A review of the literature. *International Migration Review, 18,* 237-257.

Beal, I. (2007). *A long way gone: memoirs of a boy soldier.* NY: Sarah Crichton Books.

Cowart, M. (2006). From killing fields to classrooms: Understanding and teaching the refugee student. In P. Dam & M. T. Cowart (Eds.), *Cultural and linguistic issues for English language learners* (pp.1-25). Denton, TX: Federation of North Texas Area Universities.

Delgad-Gaitan, C. (1991). Involving parents in the schools: A process of empowerment. *American Journal of Education, 100,* 20-46.

Dulay, H., Burt, M., & Krashen, S. (1982). *Language two.* NY: Oxford University Press.

Eisenbruch, M. (1988). The mental health of refugee children and their cultural development. *International Migration Review, 22,* 282-300.

Eisenbruch, M., de Jong, J.T.V.M., & van de Put, W. (2004). Bringing order out of chaos: A culturally competent approach to managing the problems of refugees and victims of organized violence. *Journal of Traumatic Stress, 17*(2), 123-131.

Gollnick, D.M., & Chinn, P.C. (2006). *Multicultural education in a pluralistic society.* Upper Saddle River, NJ: Pearson, Merrill, Prentice Hall.

How refugees come to America. Retrieved February 6, 2006 from U.S. Committee for Refugees and Immigrants at www.refugees.org.

Igoa, C. (1995). *The inner world of the immigrant child.* Mahwah, NJ: Lawrence Erlbaum Associates.

Kemp, C., & Rasbridge, L. (2004). *Refugee and immigrant health: A handbook for professionals.* Cambridge, UK: Cambridge University Press.

Nieto, S., & Bode, P. (2008). *Affirming diversity: The sociopolitical context of multicultural education.* NY: Pearson Education.

Pang, V. O. (2005). *Multicultural education: A caring-centered, reflective approach.* NY: McGraw-Hill.

Portes, A, & Rumbaut, R. (2006). *A portrait: Immigrant America.* Berkeley, CA: University of California Press.

Review of child and adolescent refugee mental health. (2003). Retrieved May 22, 2007 from National Center for Child Traumatic Stress at www.NCTSNet.org.

Rousseau, C. (1995). The mental health of refugee children. *Transcultural Psychiatric Review, 32,* 299-331.

Ung, L. (2000). *First they killed my father: A daughter of Cambodia remembers.* NY: HarperCollins Publishers.

Ung, L. (2005). *Lucky child.* NY: HarperCollins Publishers.

Warwick, I., Neville, R., & Smith, K. (2006). My life in Huddersfield: Supporting young asylum seekers and refugees to record their experiences of living in Huddersfield. *Social Work Education, 25,* (2), 129-137.

United States Committee for Refugees and Immigrants. (2005). *World refugee Survey.* Washington, DC: Author.

United States Committee for Refugees and Immigrants. (2006). *World refugee Survey.* Washington, DC: Author.

Echoes of Diversity: Adolescent Voices and Perspectives

Gina B. Anderson
Texas Woman's University
Elizabeth C. Cyr
Oklahoma State University

> *I like to meet new people because when they are from a different culture, it's like seeing your baby brother or sister for the first time; you don't know exactly who they are. All you know is their name, and it makes you want to, **need** to, know them better.*
> - Middle School Student

Introduction

As our nation's classrooms continue to increase in diversity, more attention is given to the role of the teacher as cultural mediator. Teachers must become knowledgeable about the role of culture in teaching and learning while also becoming better able to address the educational needs of students and families from diverse backgrounds. Furthermore, students must also learn how culture is formed and how to understand and handle the many intercultural interactions they are certain to encounter (Cushner, McClelland, & Safford, 2006; Gollnick & Chinn, 2006).

Cultural identity and intercultural interactions are very much a part of our students' everyday lives. Our students are challenged now more than ever to forge identities shaped by their own cultural and family traditions with those of the school and the larger community. As Carter (2006) put it, "Our socialization as racial and ethnic beings begins early in life, and much of this socialization occurs during the compulsory years of schooling, from preschool to high school, and even further during the collegiate years and beyond" (p. 304). Furthermore, racial and ethnic identities develop in the contexts of cultural forces, both individually and collectively; they are dynamic, not static; and their meanings, as expressed in schools, neighborhoods, peer groups, and families, vary across time, space, and region (Dolby, 2001; McCarthy, 1993; Yon, 2000).

Furthermore, the search for identity, considered the primary developmental task of the adolescent period, is very much affected by peers, parents, schools, and community members who contribute to the cultural and historical context in which the adolescent's identity is shaped (Blewitt & Broderick, 1999). The cultural and historical context of this identity formation is highly complex and multi-faceted. Adolescent identity is no longer about what it means to be a young woman or young man in primarily homogeneous surroundings. Adolescents today experience a bombardment of physical and emotional changes, media images, conflicting values, and economic and peer pressures in multiple languages and cultures they may be struggling to understand. Likewise, many scholars agree the flow across cultures of ideas, goods, and people is nothing new, but the current extent and speed of globalization are unprecedented. Because of increasing immigration, the outsourcing of international businesses, technology and the media, diverse peoples interact with one another more than ever (Friedman, 2000; Giddens, 2000; Hermans & Kempen, 1998; Sassen, 1998).

While scholars have identified a need for more awareness of cultural issues in the classroom, what do the students have to say? How sensitive are they in regard to cultural differences and in their interactions among their diverse peers? How do they identify themselves within their cultural, social context? We wanted to discover what the students themselves had to say and to determine if there were any similarities in their voices, stories and the current literature.

The purpose of this study was to provide insight into adolescents' perspectives of culture, diversity, and intercultural interactions. Using the voices of middle school students, qualitative methods were employed to describe, analyze, and interpret the participants' perspectives of culture and intercultural interactions. For the purposes of our article, the diversity and culture of which we speak is primarily in regard to ethnicity. In this article, we will discuss the findings of the study and the implications of those findings. The following sections will discuss the participants, setting and methodology.

Participants and setting

The participants were comprised of 90 middle level students from one middle school located in the Southwest United States. The male (n=42) and female (n=48) student participants ranged in age from 11 to 13. All participants were enrolled in either a seventh grade Social Studies or World Geography class with the same teacher. The student participants were primarily middle-class and European-American. Sixteen of the 90 students represented other ethnicities, and 8 students were displaced citizens as a result of Hurricane Katrina. Three student participants were international students.

Methodology

Qualitative methods were utilized to describe, analyze, and interpret the students' perspectives of culture and intercultural interactions. A multi-genre approach was used to collect classroom assignments over the period of one semester which included journal writing, narrative vignette, and poetic and artistic works. These assignments were disseminated as part of the teacher's pre-planned curriculum. Our study focused primarily on two questions: How do students identify culture? How comfortably do the student participants interact with others from different cultures? In order to provide insight into these questions, the classroom assignments were designed to elicit student responses on the definitions of culture, frustrations in regard to cultural differences, "minority" experiences, and accounts of what the students perceive as positive and negative intercultural interactions. These responses were then analyzed primarily by using Cushner and Brislin's (1996) Model of Cross-Cultural Interaction, a framework suggesting universally-experienced stages people undergo during unfamiliar cross-cultural encounters, and M. J. Bennett's (1993) Developmental Model of Intercultural Sensitivity (DMIS), a framework for understanding individual development and awareness along a continuum of highly ethnocentric to highly ethnorelative. The table below summarizes the stages of the DMIS (Bennett, 1986, 1993) and the graphic illustrates the developmental stages of intercultural sensitivity (Hammer & Bennett, 2003).

INTERCULTURAL UNDERSTANDING

DMIS Stage	Description
Denial	One's own culture is the only real one. Other cultures are avoided by distancing oneself emotionally and physically from the differences. Disinterest in difference is often demonstrated, although aggressiveness may occur if a difference is threatening.
Defense	One's own culture (or an adopted culture) is the only good one. Polarizations of "us" and "them" and "we" and "they" commonly occur. Issues of superiority over other cultures occur, and cultural difference is threatening.
Minimization	One assumes that his or her own cultural worldview is universally appropriate. Other cultures are trivialized or oversimplified.
Acceptance	All cultural viewpoints are equally complex. One accepts but does not necessarily agree with other cultural viewpoints although the disagreement is not based on ethnocentrism. Curiosity and respect results.
Adaptation	One's worldview begins to include concepts from other worldviews. People in this stage are able to look at the world with a new perspective and may intentionally change their behavior in order to communicate more effectively.
Integration	One's experience of self includes membership in and out of multiple cultures. Culture is defined in a number of different ways.

Development of Intercultural Sensitivity
Experience of Difference

Denial	Defense	Minimization	Acceptance	Adaptation	Integration

Ethnocentric   **Ethnorelative**
Stages   **Stages**

INTERCULTURAL UNDERSTANDING

INTERCULTURAL UNDERSTANDING

Student themes

The following sections begin with a discussion of the themes revealed and provide support with the student voices and stories.

<u>Food, languages, and faith</u>

When the students were asked to draw or write about what culture means to them, much of their work depicted or described culture as both objective and concrete (food and language) and subjective and abstract (religion). (For samples see opposite page.) Furthermore, these same identifiers were themes present in their responses in relating their positive, intercultural interactions. Cushner et al. (2006) describe the aspects of objective culture as consisting of the "visible, tangible elements of a group; that is the endless array of physical artifacts the people produce, the language they speak, the clothes they wear, the food they eat, and the decorative and ritual objects they create" (p. 66). On the other hand, aspects of subjective culture include the unseen, intangible aspects of culture, such as attitudes, learning styles, and social role status. When comparing culture to an iceberg, it is the objective culture that is the tip of the iceberg seen above water, and the remaining part of the iceberg hidden under water is the subjective. Cushner et al. (2006) further note that:

> This latter part is what concerns the ship's captain who must navigate the water and is the most meaningful (and potentially dangerous) part of culture that is continually operating at the unconscious level that shapes people's perceptions and responses to those perceptions. It is this aspect of culture that leads to most intercultural misunderstandings and requires the most emphasis in good multicultural or intercultural education. (p. 66)

Furthermore, the Minimization stage of Bennett's (1993) DMIS is the last stage still on the ethnocentric side of the continuum and is evidenced when people begin to recognize and accept superficial cultural differences such as eating customs, money, but continue to hold the belief that all human beings are essentially the same. Additionally, a common Minimization perspective is that there are universal values that apply to all people; however, these values are often projections from one's own culture (Van Hook, 2000). The following student comments demonstrate their interest in the objective, concrete characteristics of culture as well as demonstrate their ethnocentricity:

> One of our favorite things to do in our family is to find people from other countries just learning English. We like to ask them how to say different words [in their native language] and ask them about different foods. I think learning about different cultures can be a lot of fun.
>
> I would like to hang out with someone from a different culture because they could teach you their language and tell about what they do that's different from what we do.
>
> A recent interaction with a person different from me was very good. It gave me a different sense that he was different and had a cultural background that was not like me. He talked differently from me so it was hard to understand, but I did. I gained a different perspective on a different cultural background. A bad thing was that I thought that people from his country were crazy, but I figured out they're just like us.

Denial is the first ethnocentric stage of the DMIS. It is summarized as the inability to accept cultural differences as well as the purposeful grouping of oneself with others who are similar. According to Cushner et al. (2006), it is the "tendency to ignore the reality of diversity and is often characterized by well-meant, but ignorant, stereotyping and superficial statements of tolerance" (pp. 135-136). The following student quote clearly demonstrates this stage:

> I have a good friend who is from Ethiopia, so I am always asking him if he is hungry.

The last student comment in this section might demonstrate Acceptance, the first ethnorelative stage of the DMIS. Acceptance is summarized as the acknowledgment that differences do exist and are to be valued and respected (Van Hook, 2000). This stage is not ethnocentric only if one assumes that the other is equally complex and acceptable:

> I would like to hang out with someone different [than myself] because I like different things and people. It gets boring doing the same thing over and over again. I could get to try new foods and maybe even new games. They can teach you new languages. Some cultures do different things from the way we do. Some are more advanced and some are less advanced than us.

Stage 2 of Cushner and Brislin's (1996) Model of Cross-Cultural Interaction and the Minimization stage of Bennett's (1993) DMIS address the understanding of the cultural basis of unfamiliar behavior which includes religion, values, and rituals. During this stage, individuals typically try to understand another person's behavior based on their own knowledge and experiences (Van Hook, 2000). While this desire to understand is demonstrative of growth and development, and it begins to chip away at the top of the iceberg to below the surface, it is still the basis for ethnocentrism. The following four students voiced their perspectives on religion as a characteristic of culture:

INTERCULTURAL UNDERSTANDING

I am friends with someone from another culture. I think it is so cool because you get to learn about who they worship, where they go, and then you can compare it to your own life. My friend is Jewish, and she goes to a temple to worship, and she also takes a class [in a particular town].

Most of my friends are Christians, but I do have Atheist friends. Some of my friends are from different states and countries, and I think that's awesome.

Well, it would be cool and interesting to know someone from a different culture. They could come to a powwow with me and my family.

Painful proclamations and provocations

Many students voiced frustrations and oftentimes painful accounts of what it feels like to be a minority and to interact with others from different cultures. Language barriers proved to be both a major frustration and a negative intercultural experience with this particular group of student participants. Students mentioned the superiority complex of other students as another frustrating aspect of culture.

According to Cushner and Brislin's (1996) model, stage 3 is identified as Making Adjustments and Reshaping Cultural Identity. During this stage, individuals may experience personal change, become more critical, complex thinkers, and may develop more flexible perceptions of culture. When the students were asked "What does it feel like when you are the minority?" their responses were quite poignant. To broaden the definition of minority, we gave them examples such as "being a new student in a school, in a class, in a neighborhood, at a social gathering, etc." Their responses demonstrating stage 3 were as follows:

Being the minority makes you feel very aware of everything you do. It makes you feel like you are being

INTERCULTURAL UNDERSTANDING

videotaped or watched. Like every move you make is being monitored by the F.B.I. or C.I.A. I have moved a lot. It feels very weird at first. Once people get used to you, you feel alright.

>It's like everyone is staring at you.
>It's like you're dreaming, and no one is around to save you.
>It's like you can't breathe.
>It's like you stepped into the wrong room (maybe you did).
>It's like you're an ugly duckling in a pond of swans.

>It feels like everyone is staring at you. It feels like everyone thinks you are weird. Your cheeks get red and it seems like you've done something wrong. You get all stiff and frozen and you don't know what to do.

The student voices that follow speak to the issue of language differences as largely affecting their cultural interactions. While some of the students' responses are not overtly defensive, it also seems they are a bit resentful of the effort needed when they need to communicate with someone learning English. There is no mention of their attempt to speak another language or using nonverbal forms of communication. Bennett's (1993) Defense stage of the DMIS is characterized by recognition of cultural difference coupled with negative evaluations of, and sometimes aggressiveness toward, those whose culture is different from one's own:

>What makes me feel frustrated about someone from another culture is when you have to keep repeating what you just said 50 times so that they can comprehend it.

>I get frustrated when people from other cultures talk to me in a different language, and I don't know if they said something nice or mean.

INTERCULTURAL UNDERSTANDING

> Some (not all) African-Americans say things like, "He don't got his book!" or something like that. Really, we have had Language Arts for years, and they should know proper English by now. Oh well, I shouldn't complain 'cause I sometimes say, "ain't!"

The quote below demonstrates more awareness and understanding than the previous ones. According to Bennett's DMIS (1993), the student is in the Adaptation stage, the second to the last on the ethnorelative side of the continuum. Adaptation is when people begin to see culture as flexible, and they begin to communicate more effectively with others from different cultures. Moreover, they may begin to change some of their prior cultural perspectives:

> I went to a good-bye party for one of my friends. She spoke Spanish. I was the only person at the party who did not. I was feeling lonely, not sorry for myself, just lonely, because I could not understand a word. Everyone knew I did not speak Spanish. I knew that they did not mean to leave me out on purpose, but still. I gained a sense of how others may feel if I talk fast or speak in my own language.

Many students reported they were frustrated "when others think they are superior because of their culture." Denigration, derogation, and superiority are the three most common areas of Bennett's Defense stage of the DMIS (1993). Cushner et al. (2006) state that "Denigration or derogation refers to belittling or actively discriminating against another person. Superiority assumes extreme ethnocentrism to the point where one looks down on another" (p. 137). The following accounts support the feeling of superiority with the last one indicating further progress toward ethnorelativism:

INTERCULTURAL UNDERSTANDING

> The thing that frustrates me the most about people from a different culture is that sometimes they think that they're better than I am and have more freedom than me.
>
> I get frustrated when they don't agree on something because they think they are right, and their culture is "right", and I think that I am right.
>
> The only thing that would annoy me is that if they think their culture is better than mine. No culture is better than another because each one has its own good points and its own bad points.

<u>Safely sacred</u>

Finally, the students largely responded that it was just "easier and safer" to interact with students more like themselves. Also, many commented that different traditions, heritage, or religious beliefs prevent them from wanting to interact with others from different cultures. These two issues are strongly influenced by socialization and, again, are indicators of ethnocentrism. "While a certain degree of ethnocentrism serves to bind people together, it can also become a serious obstacle when those who have internalized different ideas and behaviors begin to interact with one another" (Cushner et al., 2006, p. 81). The following voices demonstrate that "same" is easier and safer:

> I think I'd rather hang out with someone like me. A person from another culture to hang out with might be hard. Hanging out to me is talking and just having a good time. A person from another culture can be fun to talk to but not much of a hang out buddy. When it is time to hang out, I prefer to go back to my "group." My friends and the people like me are my comfort, and I really enjoy spending time with them.
>
> I think I would rather hang out with someone from my own culture because when I am around people from my own

culture I tend to be more relaxed. I don't want to say something to offend them or make them mad.

I'd like to hang out with someone just like me because I don't think we'd get into any arguments or anything, and we would agree on a lot of stuff. I don't like feeling like I'm really different from someone, and I think if I was hanging out with someone from a different culture I might not agree or understand the way they think about things.

Cushner et al. (2006) claim religious identity is a common theme among Americans, and a study conducted by the Pew Research Center for the People and the Press (2002) found American adults place more importance on religion than other industrialized countries. However, the most recent study conducted by the American Religious Identification Survey found that religious identification is on the decline (2001). Schools are one of the few places where religious diversity intersects on a daily basis. The student participants have a great deal to say about how their beliefs or way of life is sacred to them, and it appears to be an issue when they are challenged by others. This demonstrates once again the Defense stage of Bennett's DMIS (1993):

What gets me frustrated about someone from a different culture is that they may be brought up differently so they may be annoying and may disagree to all the things you believe in. Or, sometimes they can make fun of what you believe and insult you.

Sometimes when someone from a different culture moves here it is because of their parents. They did not want to move and they say how they don't like the United States and that they wish they were back in their own country. It makes me so mad! Some other things that make me mad are when they brag about how something is so cool and what we have is so bad. Also, it makes me frustrated when they act like they are so dumb and that they can't do anything and that they have to have help.

What makes me feel frustrated with people from other countries is that some people use their religion or culture to be rude to other people.

In summary, the student participants' voices and stories provided the data for providing insight into their perspectives of diversity, culture, and intercultural interactions.

Discussion, limitations, and implications

Our study revealed this particular group of adolescents approaches culture, diversity, and intercultural interactions from primarily an ethnocentric perspective. In addition, they, as a collective group, demonstrate low levels of sensitivity in regard to cultural differences. This was evidenced clearly through the students' accounts of their cultural perspectives of food, language, and religion as analyzed by Bennett's (1993) Developmental Model of Intercultural Sensitivity (DMIS) and the objective aspects of culture they commonly referenced.

While these student participants clearly expressed their interest in learning more about others from diverse backgrounds, they also made judgments based on their own standards. Their moving testimonies describing their "minority experiences" lead us to believe students need more opportunities to explore their intercultural sensitivity. When they are forced to view their world through a different lens, their ethnocentrism is challenged. At the time of this study, the students' voices and comments clearly demonstrated the purposeful distancing of themselves from others who are "different."

Language differences emerged as a theme recurring in both their positive and negative interactions. The students' attitudes toward foreign languages suggest a resistance to change and a reluctance to learn a language other than English. Their attitudes are similar to those held by some in American society who believe that learning truly can begin only when English is the language of instruction. In fact the usual practice of most schools is to assist English language learners in letting go of their heritage languages as soon as possible so that learning may commence. Nieto (2008) suggests that a better approach would be to utilize heritage languages as rich personal and national resources.

Furthermore, issues related to values, beliefs, and religion were common throughout this cultural investigation. These students often identified their beliefs as having a direct relationship to their cultural identity and their intercultural relationships. Lastly, these students strongly identified with culture within their social and adolescent context. Their voices and stories were expressive and descriptive and without reserve.

Ethnocentrism is such a socializing factor that it is not uncommon for people to retain that point of view throughout their adult lives. According to Bennett (1993), the first stage, Denial, indicates inability to see cultural differences and is almost child-like in nature, with most people progressing through this first ethnocentric stage. However, many people remain in the second, Defense, and third, Minimization, stages on the ethnocentric side of the continuum. There is evidence to suggest that most teachers are at the Minimization stage and are pleased to be there because they have transcended Defense (Mahon, 2002). A danger of this stage is that it can become a matter of policy which does not recognize color or difference (Cushner et al., 2006).

INTERCULTURAL UNDERSTANDING

Personal values, beliefs, and religion largely shape the races, classes, and genders of individuals, communities, and nations, and thus our intercultural interactions. Schools are unique in that they are one of the few places where such diversity intersects on a daily basis. The first amendment to the U.S. Constitution Establishment Clause calls for a separation of church and state while the traditional American public school continues to mirror a western cultural worldview which consists of Eurocentrism, individualism, middle-class values, and generally a Protestant Christian belief system (Spring, 2003). This predominantly Protestant, Western worldview no longer mirrors our students in today's classrooms; however, it is evident that our students want and need an outlet to discuss spiritual issues.

A current summary of the research indicates most adolescents want to believe in themselves as successful persons, to be liked and respected, to do and learn things that are worthwhile, enjoy physical exercise and the freedom to move, and seek justice for themselves and others (Arnold, 1993; Beane & Lipka, 1986; Elkind, 1984; Stevenson, 2002). Their desire for respect and justice speaks clearly to the need for cultural mediation in the classroom and is supported by current literature. The student voices and stories of our study confirm the search for cultural identity within the stages of adolescent development.

While our study showed many insights into this particular group of adolescents' perspectives, it is not without limitations. First, data was collected using only one teacher's students in one middle school in the southwest area of the U.S.; therefore, the findings are not generalizable to all adolescents or middle school classrooms. Secondly, the authors and classroom teacher were female, middle-class European-Americans. It is quite likely the cross-cultural development and level of intercultural sensitivity of the authors and teacher influenced the collection and interpretation of the data. Finally, the data was not disaggregated according to the students' cultural backgrounds. Therefore, more specific data on a particular student's perspective based on his or her culture, diversity, or experiences was not gained. While this may seem as a limitation in some regards, the intent of the study was to gain insight into the collective group of adolescents as a whole rather than in specific cases.

Ideally, adolescents (and all students) would go to schools where intercultural interactions are nurtured and cross-cultural relationships are formed. While the current literature states that both can be developed and shaped within the context of a developmentally appropriate, culturally-responsive classroom (Gay, 2000; Kea, Campbell-Whatley, & Richards, 2004; Richards, Brown, & Forde, 2004; Wlodkowski & Ginsberg, 1995), the reality of this occurring may not be as commonplace as we would hope. What if the classroom teacher is still stuck in the Minimization stage? How can teachers legally and respectfully address religion as an aspect of culture without getting defensive?

Our hope is that important changes will be initiated as a result of this study. We cannot help our middle school students move beyond ethnocentrism if indeed our teachers do not. Colleges of Education (and all colleges) must help their undergraduates examine their attitudes and beliefs in order to help them recognize how ethnocentricity could affect their practice. A multicultural approach to teacher education is imperative. Kea et al. (2004) recommend that teacher educators "develop cohesive and comprehensive multicultural curricula, infuse multicultural principles throughout to prepare teachers to respond to the needs of diverse learners and their families, and identify critical teaching behaviors and essential best practices for diverse students" (p. 4).

INTERCULTURAL UNDERSTANDING

Culturally-responsive classrooms will then have a better chance of existing, and our teachers will be able to help their students move beyond Defense and Minimization.

Our study revealed religion as a primary source of cultural identification which influenced peer interactions. The implications of these results indicate a true need for schools to address this issue and to integrate religion into the curriculum as a part of the culture-learning process. A comparative approach to the study of religion both adheres to the establishment clause of the First Amendment to the Constitution of the United States and acknowledges and values the presence of religion in our students' cultural identity. Comparative studies help students develop a philosophy and possibly a new way of looking at the world around them. Additionally, comparative philosophy bridges the gap in a diverse society where a shared tradition is absent. It assumes diversity in that it presents different traditions in relation to one another without using one as a focal point (Kjellberg, 1996). This author comments:

> What students walk away with from comparative philosophy is the ability to locate different ways of looking at the world relative to one another, and the disposition to see themselves within this larger context. Our own views, after all, are what they are by virtue of their similarities to and differences from other views. The better we understand ourselves in this way, the better we understand ourselves as human beings. (p. 23)

Culturally responsive instructional strategies complement all we have proposed as a result of our study. Culturally responsive instruction addresses the needs of all learners in the classroom and helps to ensure all have equal access to academic success. Acknowledging student differences and commonalities; validating students' cultural identities in classroom practices and materials; teaching about global diversity; promoting equity and respect; utilizing valid assessments; connecting relationships between students, their families, the community, and the school; motivating students to take control of their learning; encouraging critical thinking; challenging students to strive for their own individual potential for excellence; and helping students become socially just are some specific activities to promote culturally responsive instruction (Banks & Banks, 2004; Gay, 2000; Ladson-Billings, 1994; Nieto, 1999).

Conclusion and recommendations

In summary, we recommend the following multicultural approach to teaching and learning for both teacher educators and in-service teachers based on the results of our study:
- Challenge the ethnocentric perspectives of your students and yourself;
- Model respect and appreciation of diverse languages;
- Encourage the goal of becoming bilingual;
- Explore the context of your students' (as well as your own) personal values and spiritual beliefs; and
- Integrate a comparative philosophy approach to the study of religion into the curriculum.

Our adolescent student participants care about culture and interacting among their diverse peers. However, they need a great deal of assistance navigating their way to healthy, sensitive intercultural relationships. Teachers who are ethnocentric generally find it difficult to become effective cultural mediators. Teacher education programs must integrate a multicultural approach throughout all coursework to help teachers move beyond Defense and Minimization. Teachers can then effectively utilize culturally responsive teaching strategies in their classrooms. One of those strategies is a comparative philosophy approach to the study of religion as an integral part of the culture-learning process. Once these changes take place, our adolescents will develop and thrive in our global, diverse world.

References

Arnold, J. F. (1993). A curriculum to empower young adolescents. *Midpoints, 4* (1). Columbus, OH: National Middle School Association.

Beane, J. A., & Lipka, R. P. (1986). *Self-concept, self-esteem, and the curriculum.* NY: Teachers College Press.

Bennett, M. J. (1986). A developmental approach to training for intercultural sensitivity. *International Journal of Intercultural Relations, 10* (2), 179-195.

Bennett, M. J. (1993). Towards ethnorelativism: A developmental model of intercultural sensitivity. In M. Paige (Ed.), *Cross-Cultural Orientation.* Lanham, MD: University Press of America.

Blewitt, P., & Broderick, P. C. (1999). Adolescent identity: Peers, parents, culture, and the counselor. *Counseling and Human Development, 21* (8), n. p.

Carter, P. L. (2006). Straddling boundaries: Identity, culture, and school. *Sociology of Education, 79,* 304-328.

Cushner, K., & Brislin, R. (1996). *Intercultural interactions: A practical guide* (2nd ed.). Thousand Oaks, CA: Sage.

Cushner, K., McClelland, A., & Safford, P. (2006). *Human diversity in education: An integrative approach* (5th ed.). Boston: McGraw-Hill.

Dolby, N. (2001). *Constructing race: Youth, identity, and popular culture in South Africa.* Albany: State University of New York Press.

Elkind, D. (1984). *All grown-up & no place to go: Teenagers in crisis.* Reading, MA: Addison-Wesley.

Friedman, T. L. (2000). *The lexus and the olive tree: Understanding globalization.* NY: Anchor.

Gay, G. (2000). *Culturally responsive teaching: Theory, research, and practice.* NY: Teachers College Press.

Giddens, A. (2000). *The consequences of modernity.* Cambridge, MA: Polity Press.

Gollnick, D. M., & Chinn, P. C. (2006). *Multicultural education in a pluralistic society.* Upper Saddle River, NJ: Pearson-Merrill Prentice Hall.

Hammer, M. R., & Bennett, M. J. (2003). Measuring intercultural sensitivity: The intercultural development inventory. *International Journal of Intercultural Relations, 27,* 421-443.

Hermans, H. J. M., & Kempen, H. J. G. (1998). Moving cultures: The perilous problems of cultural dichotomies in a globalizing society. *American Psychologist, 53,* 1111-1120.

Kea, C., Campbell-Whatley, G. D., & Richards, H. V. (2005). *Becoming culturally-responsive educators: Rethinking teacher education pedagogy.* Washington, DC: National Center for Culturally Responsive Systems, U.S. Department of Education.

Kjellberg, P. (1996). Multicultural education and the virtue of comparative philosophy. *Report from the Institute for Philosophy & Public Policy, 16*(3/4).

Kosmin, B. A., & Mayer, E. (2001). *American religious identification survey.* The Graduate Center of the City University of New York. Retrieved April 30, 2007 from http://www.gc.cuny.edu/faculty/research_studies/aris.pdf

Mahon, J. (2002). *The intercultural sensitivity of practicing teachers: Life history perspectives.* Unpublished doctoral dissertation, Kent State University, Ohio.

McCarthy, C. (1993). *Race, identity, and representation in education*. NY: Routledge.

Nieto, S., & Bode, P. (2008). *Affirming diversity: The sociopolitical context of multicultural education*. Boston: Pearson Education, Inc.

Pew Research Center for the People and the Press. (2002). *Among wealthy nations, U.S. stands alone in its embrace of religion*. Retrieved April 30, 2007 from http://www.religioustolerance.org/rel_impo.htm

Richards, H. V., Brown, A. F., & Forde, T. B. (2004). *Addressing diversity in schools: Culturally responsive pedagogy*. Denver, CO: National Center for Culturally Responsive Educational Systems.

Sassen, S. (1998). *Globalization and its discontents: Essays on the mobility of people and money*. NY: The New Press.

Spring, J. (2003). *American education* (11th ed.). Boston: McGraw-Hill.

Stevenson, C. (2002). *Teaching ten to fourteen year olds* (3rd ed.). Boston: Allyn & Bacon.

Van Hook, C. (2000). *Preparing teachers for the diverse classroom: A developmental model of intercultural sensitivity*. ERIC Document number 470878.

Wlodkowski, R. J., & Ginsberg, M. B. (1995). A framework for culturally responsive teaching. *Educational Leadership, 53* (1), 17-21.

Yon, D. (2000). *Elusive culture: Schooling, race, and identity in global times*. Albany: State University of New York Press.

Mother-Tongue Interference in Spanish-Speaking English Language Learners' Interlanguage

Phap Dam
Texas Woman's University

Interlanguage, or learner language, is the type of language produced by second-language learners who are in the process of learning a language. In this process, learners' errors are caused by such phenomena as borrowing patterns from the mother tongue, extending patterns from the target language, and expressing meanings using the vocabulary and syntax which are already known (Richards, Platt, & Platt, 1992).

This article is a practical reference guide that explains how Spanish-speaking English language learners make errors in their interlanguage by borrowing patterns from their mother tongue, a process referred to as "negative transfer" or "interference" by a number of researchers (James, 1980; Nobel, 1982; Swan & Smith, 1987; Brown, 2001; Parker & Riley, 1994; Horwitz, 2008). The author hopes that this guide will help teachers of Spanish-speaking English language learners anticipate the characteristic errors potentially made by this particular student population and understand how these errors arise. This information has practical pedagogical value, about which Parker and Riley (1994) commented that "the influence of L1 on L2 acquisition cannot be ignored" (p. 225), and Fillmore and Snow (2000) noted that "understanding the variety of structures that different languages and dialects use to show meaning, including grammatical meaning such as plurality or past tense, can help teachers see the errors of their students who are learning English" (p. 16).

Typical interference errors are exemplified and explained in the following areas: (1) articles, (2) gender, (3) number, (4) personal pronouns, (5) relative pronouns, (6) adjectives, (7) prepositions, (8) possessives, (9) question formation, (10) negation, (11) verb tenses, (12) passive voice, (13) word order, and (14) false cognates. The examples illustrating these interference-induced errors are from the author's own observations as well as those shared by bilingual education teachers enrolled in his graduate-level course in second-language acquisition during the past several years at Texas Woman's University. Examples containing interference errors are italicized, and below them are their correct forms and explanations for the negative transfer, illustrated by a Spanish sentence whose structure influences the interlanguage example.

1. Articles

I will read my book and the yours also.
I will read my book and yours also.
In Spanish the definite article (el, la) is used with possessive pronouns: Voy a leer mi libro y el tuyo también.

Our uncle is doctor.
Our uncle is a doctor.
In Spanish the indefinite article (un, uno, una) is not used before nouns describing profession, occupation or social status: Nuestro tío es médico.

INTERCULTURAL UNDERSTANDING

Juan is looking for one house for his parents.
Juan is looking for a house for his parents.
No distinction is made between the indefinite article (un, uno, una) and the number one (uno) in Spanish: Juan está buscando una casa para sus padres.

Can you recommend ones good books?
Can you recommend some good books?
The plural form (unos, unas) of the Spanish indefinite article (uno, una) means "some": ¿Puede recomendar unos buenos libros?

2. Gender

What bright moon! Look at her!
What bright moon! Look at it!
Grammatical gender is assigned to nouns in Spanish, in which the moon (la luna) is feminine: ¡Qué luna más brillante! ¡Mírala!

3. Number

We love hers news friends.
We love her new friends.
In Spanish, the plural marker applies not only to nouns, but also to articles, adjectives, and possessive adjectives: Queremos a sus nuevos amigos.

The other childs got lost.
The other children got lost.
There exist no irregular plural nouns in Spanish.

INTERCULTURAL UNDERSTANDING

Roberto needs a new trouser.
Roberto needs a new pair of trousers.
English words describing such "symmetrical" things as trousers and pajamas tend to be singular in Spanish: Roberto necesita un nuevo pantalón.

I owe him two hundreds dollars.
I owe him two hundred dollars.
The word for two hundred in Spanish (doscientos) ends with a plural marker: Le debo a él doscientos dólares.

4. Personal pronouns

Alberto is not from Mexico. Is from Cuba.
Alberto is not from Mexico. He's from Cuba.
Subject pronouns are frequently dropped in Spanish, which is a "pro-drop" language: Alberto no es de México. Es de Cuba.

Are many sick students in class today.
There are many sick students in class today.
Spanish does not have the equivalent for the English surrogate subject "There" found in existential sentences like "There is hope" and "There were many people at the party." According to Butt and Benjamin (2000), "In Spanish such sentences usually involve the special verb *haber* (present indicative *hay*), which means 'there is/are'" (p. 407): Hay muchos estudiantes enfermos en la clase hoy.

5. Relative pronouns

The teacher which spoke Spanish left our school.
The teacher who spoke Spanish left our school.

INTERCULTURAL UNDERSTANDING

The song who was played was romantic.
The song which was played was romantic.
No distinction is made between personal and non-personal relative pronouns in Spanish, as Butt and Benjamin (2000) noted, "Que is by far the most frequent relative pronoun and may be used in the majority of cases to translate the English relative pronouns 'who', 'whom', 'which' or 'that'" (p. 495).

6. Adjectives

He found two shirts of different colors and bought the blue.
He found two shirts of different colors and bought the blue one.
An adjective in Spanish can act as a noun after the definite article: El encontró dos camisas de diferentes colores y compró la azul.

My father is more rich than my uncle, but my grandfather is the most rich.
My father is richer than my uncle, but my grandfather is the richest.
Comparative and superlative forms of Spanish adjectives are consistently constructed with "más" and "el más," which are the equivalents of "more" and "most": Mi padre es más rico que mi tío, pero mi abuelo es el más rico de todos.

Look at these beautifuls flowers!
Look at these beautiful flowers!
In Spanish, adjectives agree with nouns that they modify: ¡Mira estas lindas flores!

INTERCULTURAL UNDERSTANDING

Everyone was boring with the principal's speech.
Everyone was bored with the principal's speech.
The Spanish adjective "aburrido" means both "boring" and "bored": Todos estaban aburridos con el discurso del director.

7. Prepositions

Who assassinated to Abraham Lincoln?
Who assassinated Abraham Lincoln?
In Spanish, the personal preposition "a" is used after a transitive verb whose direct object is human: ¿Quién asesinó a Abraham Lincoln?

For what did they come?
What did they come for?
Prepositions cannot occur at the end of a sentence in Spanish: ¿Para qué vinieron?

After to eat breakfast, we go to school.
After eating breakfast, we go to school.
An infinitive verb can follow a preposition in Spanish: Después de comer el desayuno, vamos a la escuela.

My friend and I talk by the phone all the time.
My friend and I talk on the phone all the time.
"By the phone" is the English rendition of "por teléfono": Mi amigo y yo hablamos por teléfono todo el tiempo.

The tourists finally arrived to Madrid.
The tourists finally arrived Madrid.

INTERCULTURAL UNDERSTANDING

"To Madrid" is the English rendition of "a Madrid": Los turistas finalmente llegaron a Madrid.

8. Possessives

Lisa washes the hair twice a week.
Lisa washes her hair twice a week.
In Spanish, the definite article "el" --not the possessive adjective "su"-- is used in this context: Lisa se lava el pelo dos veces por semana.

Please show us the house of Mary.
Please show us Mary's house.
The Spanish "of-phrase" is used instead of the English "possessive case": ¡Muéstrenos la casa de Mary, por favor!

9. Question formation

Has seen Mary the movie?
Has Mary seen the movie?
Spanish word order is used: ¿Ha visto Mary la película?

When John left?
John left when?
John, when left?
When did John leave?
In Spanish, word order is not fixed for questions, and there are no counterparts for the question words "do," "does," and "did."

INTERCULTURAL UNDERSTANDING

10. Negation

Roberto not found his book.
Roberto did not find his book.
There are no Spanish equivalents for "do not," "does not," and "did not" which express a verb in the negative. In Spanish, the negative particle "no" is put in front of the verb phrase, regardless of tenses or persons: Roberto no encontró su libro.

He said he did not see nobody.
He said he did not see anybody.
Double negation is standard in Spanish: Dijo que no vio a nadie. This syntactical feature makes it difficult for Spanish speakers to differentiate the three English categories of assertive forms such as "some" and "somebody," non-assertive forms such as "any" and "anybody," and negative forms such as "no" and "none" (Coe, 1987).

11. Verb tenses

Look, it snows!
Look, it's snowing!
In Spanish, the simple present tense is frequently used to express an action that is taking place at the moment of speaking. Thus, "Nieva" means both "It snows" and "It is snowing."

We see each other tomorrow.
We will see each other tomorrow.
In Spanish, the simple present tense is often used for a future action: Nos vemos mañana.

INTERCULTURAL UNDERSTANDING

I live here since 1995.
I have lived here since 1995.
In Spanish, the simple present tense can express an action that began in the past but continues to the moment of speaking: Vivo aquí desde 1992.

Come you this evening to eat with us!
Come this evening to eat with us!
In Spanish, a sentence in the imperative mood can have an expressed subject: ¡Venga usted esta noche a cenar con nosotros!

12. Passive voice

Spanish speaks itself here.
Spanish is spoken here.
"Spanish speaks itself here" is the English rendition of "Se habla español aquí," a syntactical construction used in preference to a passive sentence without the agent phrase. An agent phrase is a prepositional phrase beginning with "by" in English and "por" in Spanish, as in "Spanish is spoken here <u>by</u> the people" and "Español es hablado aquí <u>por</u> la gente." According to Nobel (1982), "passive sentences which lack the agent are not used often in Spanish" (p. 233). Nobel also noted that a special construction called the "se-passive" is used instead, and that this construction has no counterpart in English.

13. Word order

Arrived very late the teacher this morning.
This morning arrived very late the teacher.
The teacher arrived this morning very late.

INTERCULTURAL UNDERSTANDING

The teacher arrived very late this morning.

Word order is much freer in Spanish than it is in English. According to Coe (1987), "The freer word order allows words that are emphasized to be placed last" (p.79). The three interlanguage sentences listed above reflect this particular feature of Spanish, causing errors in English.

Often they have given to the church.
They often have given to the church.
They have often given to the church.

In Spanish, adverbs of frequency have several possible positions in the sentence, but not the typical central position as in English.

Juan belongs to the Club of Soccer of Dallas.
Juan belongs to the Dallas Soccer Club.

In Spanish, head nouns are typically "post-modified," in opposition to English: Juan pertenece al Club de Soccer de Dallas.

John sent to Roberto a gift.
John sent a gift to Roberto.
John sent Roberto a gift.

In Spanish, an indirect object must have a preposition such as "a," and the direct object and indirect object can go in either order. The English two-object structure without a preposition (John sent Roberto a gift) is unfamiliar to Spanish speakers and they may avoid it (Coe, 1987).

Felipe took to school his favorite books.
John took his favorite books to school.

INTERCULTURAL UNDERSTANDING

In Spanish, a preposition phrase is regularly put in front of a direct object: Felipe llevó a la escuela sus libros favoritos.

Our teacher speaks very well English and Spanish.
Our teacher speaks English and Spanish very well.
In Spanish, an adverbial phrase is regularly put in front of a direct object: Nuestra maestra habla muy bien inglés y español.

14. False cognates

Spanish originates from Latin; therefore, its vocabularies correspond with the Latin-derived side of the English language (Coe, 1987). These corresponding vocabularies are known as cognates. As Crandall, Dias, Gingras, and Harris (1981) warned, "Cognates can be both a blessing and a curse for the teachers and learners of a second language" (p. 49). Indeed, while these thousands of cognates can help Spanish-speaking English language learners accelerate their acquisition of English vocabulary, some of them are "false friends" and deserve to be pointed out for the benefit of the learners. Examples of interference errors due to false cognates are given below.

Every child should assist to school.
Every child should attend school.
In Spanish, "asistir a la escuela" means "to attend school."

Take me to a library. I need to buy some books there.
Take me to a bookstore. I need to buy some books there.
In Spanish, "librería" means "bookstore."

INTERCULTURAL UNDERSTANDING

Mrs. Gonzalez was a professor in a high school in South America.
Mrs. Gonzalez was a high-school teacher in South America.
In many Spanish-speaking countries, "profesor" means "teacher" of any school, from elementary school to university.

My friend was constipated. He took a Comtrex tablet and felt better.
My friend had a head cold. He took a Comtrex tablet and felt better.
The Spanish adjective "constipado" means "suffering from a cold" and has nothing to do with difficult evacuation of the bowels.

Our instructor can speak several idioms.
Our instructor can speak several languages.
The Spanish noun "idioma" means "language."

After a long vacation, it's hard to regress to school.
After a long vacation, it's hard to return to school.
The Spanish verb "regresar" means "return."

In addition to the previously-mentioned supporting comments by Parker and Riley (1994) and Fillmore and Snow (2000) on the benefits of teachers' ability to anticipate the characteristic interference-induced errors made by English language learners, the author believes that knowing the reasoning behind certain errors should be part of the teacher's role as monitor and assessor of the learner's output. As James (1980) eloquently put it, "It is on the basis of such diagnostic knowledge that the teacher organizes feedback to the learner and remedial work. Even the learner should know why he has committed errors if he is to self-monitor and avoid these same errors in the future" (p. 148).

References

Brown, H.D. (2001). *Teaching by principles: An interactive approach to language Pedagogy.* White Plains, NY: Longman.

Butt, J., & Benjamin, C. (2000). *A new reference grammar of modern Spanish.* Lincolnwood, IL: NTC Publishing Group.

Coe, N. (1987). Speakers of Spanish and Catalan. In M. Swan & B. Smith (Eds.), *Learner English* (pp. 72-89). Cambridge, England: Cambridge University Press.

Crandall, J.A., Dias, J., Gingras, R.C., & Harris, T.K. (1981). *Teaching the Spanish-speaking child.* Englewood Cliffs, NJ: Prentice Hall Regents.

Dam, P., De la Ossa, E., Garcia, A.C, Graham, N., Hong-Fincher, B., Kim, S., et al. (2004). *Teacher's resource guide of language transfer issues for English language learners.* Barrington, IL: Rigby.

Fillmore, L.W., & Snow, C.E. (2000). *What teachers need to know about language.* Washington, DC: US Department of Education.

Horwitz, E.K. (2008). *Becoming a language teacher.* Boston: Pearson.

James, C. (1980). *Contrastive analysis.* Essex, England: Longman Group UK Limited.

Nobel, B.L. (1982). *Linguistics for bilinguals.* Rowley, MA: Newbury House Publishers.

Parker, F., & Riley, K. (1994). *Linguistics for non-linguists.* Needham Heights, MA: Allyn and Bacon.

Richards, J.C., Platt, J., & Platt, H. (Eds.). (1992). *Longman dictionary of language Teaching & applied linguistics.* Essex, England: Longman Group UK Limited.

Selinker, L. (1992). *Rediscovering interlanguage.* New York: Longman, Inc.
Swan, M., & Smith, B. (1987). *Learner English.* Cambridge, England: Cambridge University Press.

Factors Affecting English Language Learners' Acquisition of English: Implications for English Language Institutes

Emily Chou
Chihlee Institute of Technology, Taiwan

Introduction

Since 1998 the number of international students who are non-English native speakers choosing to study in the United States has declined (Institute of International Education, 2004). This decline in enrollment is significant because in the past international students have brought in over $13 billion dollars to the American economy through money spent on tuition, living expenses, and related cost. According to a survey by the Institute of International Education in 2004, nearly 75% of all international students reported that the money they spent in the United States was from personal and family sources or other sources outside of the United States. With statistics like these, educators and policymakers are seeking to find the best ways to reach international students and recruit more of them to study in the United States. In order to find the best ways to reach these international students and recruit them, it is important to ascertain their needs as a means for finding ways to help them meet language proficiency requirements in the United States.

Most post-high school international students who are English language learners (ELLs) come to the United States primarily to continue their academic studies at a college, university or technical institute. Some students may specifically focus on improving their

English communication skills. Regardless of the reason these ELLs come to the United States, one main obstacle they face is that of language proficiency. Since language proficiency is such a key factor for these international students' adjustment to life in the United States, a question arises about how language institutes and their instructors might help ELLs improve their English skills. One way to answer this question is to investigate ELLs' perspectives about language learning in order to help these international students improve their English skills. Gaining these international students' perspectives about learning English would add insight to the current understanding of the needs of English language learners, since they are the ones subjectively experiencing the learning process. By focusing on students' perspectives, this study attempts to discover how ELLs think and feel about their experience of language learning. Through analyzing factors that contribute to language learning experience, the director and the instructors in the language institutes will better understand the needs of ELLs and be better equipped to ensure that all these international students learn English effectively.

The research literature related to language learning has focused on a variety of factors affecting English language learning (Gardner & Lambert, 1972; Horwitz, 1988; Oxford, 1990). The first area of this study has focused on learners' motivation. A number of studies have identified the important role that motivation plays in learning a second language (Gardner & Lambert, 1972; Clément & Kruidenier, 1985; Dornyei, 1990; Ely, 1986; Scarcella & Oxford, 1992). Motivated learners learn more because they seek input, interaction, and instruction. When motivated learners encounter input in the target language, they tend to pay attention to it and actively process it.

INTERCULTURAL UNDERSTANDING

A second area of research has targeted the beliefs that the language learners hold about learning a second language (Crookes & Schmidt, 1991; Tremblay & Gardner, 1995). Second language learners may believe that one's aptitude or the difficulty of the language contributes to or hampers their learning of the language (Horwitz, 1987).

A third area of research has examined the learning strategies that the language learners use while learning a second language. Successful language learners use more learning strategies than poor language learners (Rubin, 1975; Stern, 1975; Oxford, 1990).

A fourth area of research has suggested that learning environment, both at home and in school, plays a significant role for children's literacy development (Diamond & Moore, 1990; Teale, 1986; Heath, 1983; Rasinski & Padak, 1996). This same view has been applied to adult English language learners. The role of the home learning environment, the classroom learning environment, and even the social setting outside the classroom learning environment have been found to be contributing factors to ELLs' language learning progress.

A fifth area of research has shown that language acquisition occurs more easily when the linguistic distance between the first language and the target language is less (Chomsky, 1986; Flynn & Martohardjono, 1995; White, 1989). Linguistic distance refers to the differences in the meaning, the structure, and the use of words between the first language and the target language. For instance, English is linguistically closer to Western European languages, such as French and German, than it is to East Asian languages, such as Korean and Japanese. It would be expected that Western European students have less learning burden than students from East Asia.

INTERCULTURAL UNDERSTANDING

Collectively, research related to English language learning suggests a variety of factors may contribute to language learning. For instance, a learner's motivation and beliefs about language learning may affect his/her choice of learning strategies and ultimately affect his/her language proficiency. The fact that existing research has attempted to isolate factors, such as motivation, beliefs, or learning strategies, ignores the complexity of the language learning process. While much is known about how each factor contributes individually to the students' language learning, little is known about the relationships among the factors. Thus studies that explore the relationship among factors are needed in order to identify how ELLs can learn effectively.

The purpose of this study is to survey the importance of various factors related to language learning from the perspective of ELLs and to determine the relationships among these factors which affect ELLs' language learning and their language proficiency. Specifically, what do ELLs perceive to be the important factors contributing to their language learning and what are the relationships among the factors affecting ELLs' language learning and their language proficiency?

This study was conducted at English language institutes in the United States, because these English language institutes are often the first phase for international students to receive academic experience in the United States. An English language institute may be either college/university-affiliated or may operate as an independent, private program. Usually these language institutes offer intensive English programs for international students to improve their English skills within a relatively short period of time. These intensive English programs are usually about four hours or more per day of class time, five days a week.

Sample size for the study was determined by recommended statistical sampling and length of questionnaire size. It was recommended that sample size be four to ten times the number of items on the questionnaire (Cattell, 1978; Gorsuch, 1983; Tanaka, 1987). Accordingly, this study required 172 to 430 respondents to accommodate the 43 items in the questionnaire. In order to obtain enough respondents for this study, the researcher sent an invitation letter via email to all 273 English language institutes on the American Association of Intensive English Programs list. The language institutes that were willing to participate in this study received a package which included a letter explaining the purpose of this study and copies of the self-developed questionnaire. Also, the directors of the language institutes who were willing to participate would use the appropriate school letterhead to return the agreement letter to the researcher.

The international students from those language institutes were invited to complete a questionnaire. Following the completion and return of the questionnaires, only the respondents who reported their Test of English as a Foreign Language (TOEFL) score were included in this study. This was necessary since the TOEFL score was used as the dependent variable to identify ELLs' language proficiency. The researcher included the responses from respondents whose levels of English competency were in the middle or above at language institutes instead of the lower level to assure comprehension of the questionnaire. The respondent's TOEFL score and his/her level of English competency formed the basis of choosing questionnaires valid to this research project.

The design of the questionnaire instrument was critical for discovering what ELLs perceived as important aspects of learning English. With this purpose in mind, the researcher examined several existing questionnaires from past research, but could not find an appropriate one for the purpose of this study. The existing research was focused on one single language learning factor individually, and does not consider the complexity of the language learning process. Questionnaires that were reviewed but found not to be appropriate for the study included *"Support vs: Challenge in Classroom Interaction," "The Attitude/Motivation Test Battery," "Beliefs About Language Learning Inventory (BALLI)," "College and University Classroom Environment Inventory* (CUCEI)" and *"Strategy Inventory for Language Learning (SILL)."*

After reviewing the existing questionnaires, the researcher believed that there was a need to develop a questionnaire which considered the complexity of the language learning process. The questionnaire for this study contained two sections. Section I covered demographic information, including age, gender, personal background, and English proficiency of the respondents (TOEFL score). Section II consisted of 43 statements about various factors related to language learning. All statements in the questionnaire requested the respondents to indicate on a five-point scale (1 = strongly disagree to 5 = strongly agree) their thoughts about the language they were currently learning, in this case English.

Pilot testing is important for establishing content validity by assurance that the items are really measuring what they are intended to measure (Creswell, 2003). In regards to selecting groups to determine content validity of a given instrument, Dillman (1978) suggested that a survey should be examined by three types of people: colleagues, people who might use the data, and persons drawn from the same group as the study population. Accordingly, the researcher developed a draft questionnaire which was carefully reviewed by three experts, dissertation committee members, and students from the sample group. Recommendations from the various field review sources were included in the revision of the final questionnaire instrument. Once the initial draft questionnaire was completed, a four-phase validation process was completed as follows.

The first phase was giving the first draft of the questionnaire to ten English language learners who were studying at an English language institute. This pilot study was conducted to check the clarity of the questions and instructions on the questionnaire. There were two questions at the end of the questionnaire: 1) Is it difficult or easy to understand this questionnaire? 2) How long did it take you to finish this questionnaire? The comments from ten students indicated that the questionnaire was easy to read and understand, and took five to ten minutes to complete. Based on the feedback, revisions were made and some questions were added to each of the five factors in order to get more detailed information from the respondents.

The second phase of the validation process was to give the second draft of the questionnaire to the researcher's dissertation committee members to review. Some suggestions were provided by the committee members, such as avoiding using a conditional clause in the wording of the questions. After the questionnaire was reviewed in-depth by the committee members, the questions were revised a third time.

The third phase of the validation process was to request an independent review from three experts in the field of second language acquisition to refine and clarify the statements in the questionnaire. After editing the questions for proper word choice and clarification for the true intent of the items according to the three experts' feedback, the researcher refined the statements and arranged them in random order to account for any order effects.

The fourth phase of the validation process was to give the fourth draft of the questionnaire to the researcher's dissertation committee members for final review before sending out to English language institutes. On the final questionnaire, six statements focused on ELLs' motivations to learn a language. Eleven statements focused on respondents' beliefs about learning a language, and eight statements addressed students' learning strategies. There are twelve statements that covered students' learning environments, and lastly, six statements were related to the linguistic distance between the students' first language and English.

The researcher collected the data in the late summer and early fall of 2006. Data from each language institute willing to participate were collected in two phases. In the first phase, the researcher wrote an invitation letter to all 273 language institutes via email from the American Association of Intensive English Program list. Of the 273 language institutes, 25 language institutes responded to the email saying that they were interested in this study and the director of each language institute would need to review the questionnaire before initiating the study. Five language institutes were dropped because of the time required to answer the questionnaire. Thus, the remaining 20 institutes comprised the majority of the study. They represent fourteen states: Colorado, Florida, Georgia, Illinois, Indiana, Kansas, Kentucky, Nevada, New York, Ohio, Oklahoma, Oregon, Washington, and Utah.

In the second phase, each of these 20 language institutes was sent via the post office a package of questionnaires with a cover letter explaining the purpose of the study. Individual questionnaire instruments were identified with a numeric code so that the respondents were anonymous and could not be identified. Each language institute administered the questionnaires with its own staff, placed them in the self-addressed, stamped envelopes provided by the researcher, and mailed them back to the researcher within two weeks. The administration of the questionnaire was very flexible depending on the situation at each language institute. Some language institutes distributed the questionnaire in the computer lab or in the conversation class. Other language institutes administered the questionnaire in controlled settings such as a class session or at the testing place. In any case, answering the questionnaire was voluntary.

One thousand copies of the questionnaire were distributed to 20 English language institutes from June 2006 to September 2006. Six hundred and thirty students answered the questionnaire. Among them, 74 respondents' responses were discarded because the Test of English as a Foreign Language (TOEFL) score was unidentifiable or the questionnaire was incomplete, thus yielding 606 viable questionnaires. So, the response rate for this present study was 60.6%.

Results

What do ELLs perceive to be the important factors contributing to their language learning? To explore ELLs' perceptions of important factors contributing to their language learning, data were analyzed and were shown in Table 1. Mean score was 4.27 for beliefs about language learning, 4.24 for the learning environment subscale, 3.97 for learning strategies, 3.48 for motivation about language learning, and 3.06 for linguistic distance. That means that the respondents had the greatest importance ratings for beliefs about language learning scale, followed by the learning environment subscale, learning strategies, motivation about language learning, and linguistic distance. Accordingly, ELLs perceived that their beliefs about language learning were the most important factor contributing to their language learning.

Table 1
Average Scores for Five Factors

	N	Mean	SD	Min	Max
Beliefs about Language Learning	606	4.27	0.54	1.17	5
Learning Environment	606	4.24	0.53	1.0	5
Learning Strategies	606	3.97	0.47	1.43	5
Motivation about Language Learning	606	3.48	0.65	1.20	5
Linguistic Distance	606	3.06	0.83	1.0	5

What are the relationships between these factors and ELLs' language proficiency? The results of the multiple regression, using the five factors as predictor variables and ELLs' language proficiency as a criterion variable, were that two of the five factors, learning strategies and linguistic distance, contributed significantly to the prediction of ELLs' language proficiency (See Table 2). That is, learning strategies was the most important effect on ELLs' language proficiency (Beta = .166), and linguistic distance was the second most important effect on ELLs' language proficiency, but it is negative (Beta = -.106).

Table 2

Multiple Regression Analyses of Learning Environment, Learning Strategies, Motivation, Beliefs, and Linguistic Distance on ELLs' Language Proficiency

Predictor	Model 1		Model 2	
	Unstandardized B	Beta β	Unstandardized B	Beta β
Age	.770	.116**	.648	.098*
Learning Environment			.09	.001
Learning Strategies			12.77	.166**
Motivation			-4.63	-.085
Beliefs			1.20	.018
Linguistic Distance			-4.57	-.106**
R^2	.020		.060	
F	6.245**		5.498**	
N	606		606	

Note: * $p < .05$, ** $p < .01$

ELLs' language proficiency was mediated by the relationships among their learning strategies and linguistic distance between their first language and English. In other words, controlling for the other subscales, as rating the importance on learning strategies increased a unit, TOEFL scores increased 12.77 points ($B = 12.77$, $p < .01$). Controlling for the other subscales, as rating the importance on linguistic distance increased, TOEFL scores decreased ($B = -4.57$, $p < .01$). Accordingly, ELLs' language proficiency could be predicted from their learning strategies and linguistic distance between their first language and English. In other words, the relationships between ELLs' language proficiency and their learning strategies as well as their linguistic distance were strong.

Implications

Exploring ELLs' perspectives yielded information that can be utilized by English language institute teachers, and that can further our understanding of the complexity of the language learning process. Selected recommendations are provided below.

Recommendations for directors at English language institutes

Based on the findings in this study, some implications for the directors at English language institutes are suggested. First, the ELLs' living environment for language learning in the United States is a critical factor. It is important to have an appropriate living environment for ELLs in order to apply the language that they have learned in their daily lives. An example would be for them to live with native speakers in a dormitory to practice the language rather than living by themselves in an apartment with the friends who speak the same native language. ELLs would then have opportunities to interact directly with people who know how the language works and how it can be used (Wong Fillmore, 1991) to build linguistic proficiency.

Second, language institute directors may want to provide opportunities for students to communicate with native speakers as a criterion for program quality. An example of a program design includes inviting graduate students majoring in English as a second language into the classroom to pair up with advanced students at English language institutes in conversation and writing classes. As for the beginning and intermediate students, they can learn from the more advanced students of students of English language institutes. Accordingly, all the students at English language institutes have opportunities to interact with the people who are more competent in English. In this learning process, ELLs receive help from students proficient in English and make strides during their learning process (Vygotsky, 1978).

The findings in this study concerning learners' beliefs about language learning and ELLs' learning strategies in their learning environment provide directors at English language institutes in the United States with more knowledge about language learning from the perspective of English language learners. Such knowledge empowers them to make better decisions regarding the curriculum design as well as creating a meaningful learning environment for English language learners.

Recommendations for the teachers at English language institutes

Based on the findings in this study, some pedagogical implications for the teachers at English language institutes are suggested. First, it is important to make students aware of their own learning process and all the learning strategies actually available to them. In order for students to learn to use learning strategies, teachers should emphasize two areas. The first area focuses on teaching learning strategies that accelerate ELLs' language learning, such as how to make the connection between the new concepts with the things that learners already know. The second area focuses on assisting students to explore the strategies proven to be beneficial but used infrequently. These strategies include practicing English by making use of new language input as well as by constantly writing and speaking the language.

Second, it is necessary that teachers enrich the learning environment in the classroom by offering more opportunities for students to learn, use, and practice English. Moreover, activities which allow students to practice English outside the classroom help them to develop communicative competence. It is important to note that most of the respondents did not speak English at home and therefore required additional chances to enhance their pragmatic communicative competence.

Finally, English language learners need to be better informed about the availability of English materials and given easy access to such materials outside classroom contact hours. This study and others (e.g., Green & Oxford, 1995) have found that more proficient learners contact other sources outside the classroom for improving their language skills, such as watching TV and films in the target language, listening to the radio in the target language, and reading materials in the target language. Therefore, providing ELLs with easy access to authentic input in English via various means, both in and especially outside the classroom, can lead to increased motivation and more positive attitudes towards language learning.

References

Cattell, R. B. (1978). *Scientific use of factor analysis in behavioral and life sciences.* New York: Plenum.
Chomsky, N. (1986). *Knowledge of language: Its nature, origins, and use.* New York: Praeger.
Clément, R., & Kruidenier, B.G. (1985). Aptitude, attitude and motivation in second language proficiency: A test of

Clément's model. *Journal of Language and Social Psychology, 4,* 21-38.

Creswell, J. W. (2003). Research design: qualitative, quantitative and mixed methods approaches. Thousand Oaks, CA: Sage.

Crookes, G., & Schmidt, R.W. (1991). Motivation: Reopening the research agenda. *Language Learning, 41*(4), 469-512.

Diamond, B. J., & Moore, M. A. (1990). *Multicultural literacy: Mirroring the reality of the classroom.* New York: Longman.

Dillman, Don A. (1978). *Mail and telephone surveys: The total design method.* New York: John Wiley and Sons.

Dörnyei, Z. (1990). Conceptualizing motivation in foreign-language learning. *Language Learning, 40* (1), 45-78.

Ely, C.M. (1986). Language learning motivation: A descriptive and causal analysis. *Modern Language Journal, 70*(1), 28-34.

Flynn, S., & Martohardjono, G. (1995). Toward theory-driven language pedagogy. In F. R. Eckman, D. Highland, P. W. Lee, J. Mileham, & R. R. Weber. (Eds.), *Second language acquisition theory and pedagogy* (pp. 45-60). Mahwah, NJ: Lawrence Erlbaum Associates.

Gardner, R., & Lambert, W. (1972). *Attitudes and motivations in second language learning.* Rowley, MA: Newbury House.

Green, J. M., & Oxford, R. (1995). A closer look at learning strategies, L2 proficiency, and gender. *TESOL Quarterly, 29*(2), 261-297.

Gorsuch, R. L. (1983). *Factor analysis* (2nd ed.). Hillsdale, NJ: Lawrence Erlbaum Associates.

Heath, S. B. (1983). *Ways with words: Language, life, and work in communities and classrooms.* New York: Cambridge University Press.

Horwitz, E. K. (1987). Survey student beliefs about language learning. In A.L. Wenden, & J. Rubin. (Eds.), *Learner strategies in language learning.* Englewood Cliffs, NJ: Prentice- Hall.

Horwitz, E. K., 1988. The beliefs about language learning of beginning university foreign language students. *Modern Language Journal, 72,* 283-294.

Institute of International Education. (2004). *Open doors 2004: International students in the U.S.* New York: Institute of International Education.

Oxford, R. L. (1990). *Language learning strategies: What every teacher should know.* New York: Newbury House.

Rasinski, T., & Padak, N. (1996). *Holistic reading strategies: Teaching children who find reading difficult.* Englewood Cliffs, NJ: Prentice.

Rubin, J. (1975). What the "good language learner" can teach us. *TESOL Quarterly, 9*(1), 41-51.

Scarcella, R. C., & Oxford, R. L. (1992). *The tapestry of language learning.* Boston, MA: Heinle & Heinle Publishers.

Stern, H. H. (1975). What can we learn from the good language learner? *Canada Modern Language Review, 31*(4), 304-318.

Tanaka, S. T. (1987). "How big is big enough?" Sample size and goodness of fit in structural equation models with latent variables. *Child Development, 58*, 134-146.

Teale, W. H. (1986). Home background and young children's literacy development. In W.H. Teale & E. Sulzby (Eds.), *Emergent literacy: Writing and reading.* Norwood, NJ: Ablex Publishing Corp.

Tremblay, P. F., & Gardner, R. C. (1995). Expanding the motivation construct in language learning. *The Modern Language Journal, 79*, 505-520.

Vygotsky, L. S. (1978). *Mind in society: The development of higher psychological processes.* London: Harvard University Press.

White, L. (1989). *Universal grammar and second language acquisition.* Amsterdam, PA: John Benjamins.

Wong Fillmore, L. (1991). Second language learning in children: A model of language learning in social context. In E. Bialystock (Ed.), *Language processing in bilingual children* (pp. 49-69). New York: Cambridge University Press.

Using Cognitive Academic Language Proficiency (CALP) Scores to Enhance Educational Decision-Making for Students from Language Minority Backgrounds

Lloyd Kinnison
Texas Woman's University
Tammy L. Stephens
University of Texas at Tyler
Phillip Stager
Texas Woman's University
Jessica A. Rueter
Texas Woman's University

The demographic makeup of America's schools has changed immensely over the past decade (Fuller, Miller, & Dominguez, 2006). Santos, Corso, and Maude (2006) reported a growing diversity of children within the United States across ethnic, linguistic, socioeconomic, and ability characteristics. The increase in educational enrollment of diverse students has nearly doubled since the 22% reported in 1972 to the 43% reported in 2003 (Livingston & Wirt, 2005). The former director of the Office of Bilingual Education and Minority Language Affairs within the U.S. Department of Education, Eugene E. Garcia, reported similar findings in his 2001 publication *Hispanic Education in the United States.* He reported that K-12 public school enrollment for non-white and Hispanic students sharply increased from 10 million in 1976 to more than 20 million today (Garcia, 2001). Garcia's projections also revealed that by the year 2026 this figure will more than double to nearly 45 million. This phenomenon is also evident in Texas where 45% of the students enrolled in Texas schools during the 2004-2005 school year were Hispanic and 14% were African-American (Texas Education Agency, 2005).

The dramatic shift in ethnic and cultural diversity presents a new set of challenges at every level of our educational system. As a result of such changes in today's school population, teachers are expected to effectively teach students from an array of diverse backgrounds in ethnicity, native language, ability level, and socioeconomic status. This frequently results in a difficult task for teachers because many of these students enter school with an inability to speak and/or understand the English language (Lamb, Ochoa, & Garcia De Alba, 2006). Effectively meeting the educational requirements of such learners requires knowledge of language and culture and their impact on learner success. Unfortunately, many times the attributes of language and culture are overlooked and/or misunderstood. In turn, the lack of knowledge often results in children being misdiagnosed and inappropriately referred for special education services.

The purpose of this paper is to provide educators with a description of two types of language as identified by Cummins (1989): Basic Interpersonal Communication Skills or BICS (social language) and Cognitive Academic Language Proficiency or CALP (abstract specialized language for academic tasks). The article will also provide a brief description of language development while describing the instructional and cultural implications associated with the assessment and promotion of each type of language. Additionally, the authors will argue that the assessment of BICS and CALP domains for all non-native English speaking students referred for intervention must give additional consideration to these two language domains. Finally, the authors will conclude with a discussion regarding the utilization of BICS and CALP levels when planning instruction for language minority students.

Language acquisition

Language acquisition impacts learning. Language, a vital and complex foundational skill needed for academic success (Mercer & Mercer, 1998), is defined as a socially shared code used to represent concepts through the use of random symbols and rules governing the combinations of symbols. Rosberry-McKibbin (2007) defines language as a means whereby we communicate with others. When considering language acquisition, language can be broken into two major domains: Basic Interpersonal Communication Skills (BICS) or social language and Cognitive Academic Language Proficiency (CALP) or academic language, a distinction which is often misunderstood by educators.

Traditionally, school personnel have focused on BICS and CALP when working with English language learners (ELLs). Although the acquisition of BICS and CALP is deemed to be a top priority when planning instruction for second language learners, some educators are unable to differentiate between these two types of language. In order for classroom teachers to provide effective instruction for all students, educators need to understand how the two categories of language differ. Experts such as Jim Cummins (1984) have provided research in an attempt to differentiate between BICS and CALP.

Basic interpersonal communication skills (BICS)

BICS has been defined as language skills which are needed in social situations. BICS is often referred to as "playground language" (Cummins, 2006) because language minority learners utilize BICS skills when they are on the playground, in the lunch room, at parties, on the school bus, or playing sports. Social interactions occur in meaningful social contexts and are therefore usually context-imbedded. Furthermore, BICS is cognitively less demanding, does not require specialized language, and usually develops within six months to two years after students arrive in the U.S. (Rosberry-McKibbin, 2007).

BICS generally develops quickly among immigrant second language learners because this form of communication is supported by interpersonal and contextual cues and places relatively few cognitive demands on the individual (Cummins, 1984). However, although a student may demonstrate mastery in BICS, it should not be assumed that the student will also achieve the same degree of mastery in academic language skills. Unfortunately, a common misconception among educators is the assumption that a student who demonstrates success in expression in social situations will also be able to complete equivalent grade-level academic language tasks with similar success. This misunderstanding of BICS and CALP acquisition often results in an unusually disproportionate number of minority referrals for special education services for what appears to be the result of poor academic performance when it is actually due to a lack of sufficient exposure to English and not a true learning disability (Rhodes, Ochoa, & Ortiz, 2005).

Cognitive academic language proficiency (CALP)

While BICS addresses social language, CALP refers to formal academic learning which includes listening, speaking, reading, and writing about subject area material (Cummins, 2006; Rosberry-McKibbin, 2007). Students must demonstrate effectiveness in CALP proficiency in order to succeed in school. Demonstrating proficiency in academic language acquisition takes longer to achieve than BICS; proficiency in CALP usually takes between five to seven years. However, research has found that it may take seven to ten years for ELLs to catch up to their peers if the child has no prior schooling or is simply not provided with the appropriate support system in native language development (Rosberry-McKibbin, 2007).

It is important for teachers to understand that academic language acquisition is more than just the understanding of content area vocabulary. CALP also includes skills involving comparing, classifying, synthesizing, evaluating, and inferring information (Cummins, 1984). Additionally, academic language tasks are context-reduced, where information is read from textbooks or presented by the teacher. As a student gets older and progresses through the grades, academic tasks become more cognitively demanding and more context-reduced (Cummins, 2006).

Differentiating between BICS and CALP is an important aspect of teaching diverse learners. Educators must understand that proficiency in BICS does not necessarily translate into proficiency in CALP. The results of a misinterpretation of this concept were demonstrated through research which found that in the U.S., language minority students have frequently been assessed using IQ tests administered in English after only two or three years in the country, resulting in placement in special education classes entirely based on these test results. Moreover, research reported in the early 1980s in Texas revealed an alarming overrepresentation of Hispanic students in special education. More than three times as many Hispanic students were labeled as having learning disabilities when compared with the general school population (Ortiz & Yates, 1983).

Anderson (1997) provided considerations for evaluation of the second language student, among which is the statement that "The average student from the lower socio-economic areas is below average compared to the general norm in oral language" (p. 1). He also suggested that these students are functioning approximately one standard deviation below the average in the second language. Such a deficit acts as a barrier to grade level functioning. Anderson (1997) recommended that any assessment must consider regional variations in both the first and second languages. Finally, Anderson (2004) outlined a series of steps to be taken to insure that cognitive or educational evaluations give full consideration to the differences in the students' BICS and CALP proficiencies. In this document, he outlined various specific assessment suggestions by grade levels to insure second language issues did not interfere with considerations for special education services.

Computation and interpretation of CALP levels

CALP levels provide important information regarding a student's formal academic learning performance in the areas of listening, speaking, reading and writing (Cummins, 2006; Rosberry-McKibbin, 2007). Through the utilization of the cognitive assessment, *Woodcock-Johnson III Tests of Cognitive Abilities*, and the achievement assessment, *Woodcock-Johnson Tests of Achievement*, the assessor is able to retrieve several scores in relation to student performance. Standard scores are most prominently used when determining student eligibility for special education services (e.g., learning disability and mental retardation). However, other scores derived from student performance can also be helpful in determining levels of oral language proficiency and assist in making eligibility decisions. Such scores include the Oral Language Relative Proficiency Index (RPI) and Cognitive Academic Language Proficiency (CALP) levels.

The RPI score derived from the results of a student's performance on the Woodcock-Johnson III assessments provides a prediction of a student's degree of proficiency in comparison to same age or grade peers in the area of oral language. Specifically, Riverside Publishing defines RPI as "a score that predicts a subject's degree of proficiency in comparison to age or grade peers. It describes the quality of the performance or functionality. A subject's performance is compared to the point at which average students in the comparison group (either age or grade) would perform similar tasks with 90% proficiency. An RPI of 70/90 means a student could be expected to demonstrate with 70% proficiency what an average student in the comparison group could perform with 90% proficiency" (Riverside Publishing, 2007).

When interpreting the results of the Woodcock-Johnson III for English language proficiency, CALP rates can be obtained by computing clusters of test scores. These scores can then be used in determining whether a student actually has a disability or inadequate first or second language acquisition. Table 1 presents the cluster-combinations of tests which can be used in determining CALP levels.

Table 1.
Tests of the WJ-III used in Determining CALP Levels

WJ-III Test	Clusters Utilized for CALP Levels

Cognitive Battery:	Verbal Ability (Standard)
	  – Test 1: Verbal Comprehension
	Verbal Ability (Extended)
	  - Test 1: Verbal Comprehension, Test 11 General Information
	Comprehension Knowledge
	  - Test 1: Verbal Comprehension, Test 11 General Information

Achievement Battery:	Oral Language (Standard)
	  - Test 3 Story Recall, Test 4 Understanding Directions
	Oral Language (Extended)
	  - Test 3 Story Recall, Test 4 Understanding Directions, Test 15 Oral Comprehension
	Oral Comprehension
	  - Test 3 Story Recall, Test 14 Picture Vocabulary
	Listening Comprehension
	  - Test 4 Understanding Directions, Test 15 Oral Comprehension
	Broad Reading
	  - Test 1 Letter Word Identification, Test 2 Reading Fluency, Test 9 Passage Comprehension
	Broad Written Language
	  - Test 7 Spelling, Test 8 Writing Fluency, Test 11 Writing Samples
	Reading Comprehension
	  - Test 9 Passage Comprehension, and Test 17 Reading Vocabulary
	Written Expression
	  - Test 8 Writing Fluency and Test 11 Writing Samples
	Academic Knowledge
	  - Test 19 Academic Knowledge

Adapted from Riverside Publishing (2007)

Once RPI and CALP levels are obtained using WJ-III clusters, the assessor should use the information to interpret the student's levels and what their performance levels mean in association with English proficiency levels and the difficulty levels students will find English learning tasks. Table 2 presents information regarding the relationship between Oral Language RPI scores, CALP levels, English proficiency levels, and the difficulty level of an assigned English language task (Hebert, 2005).

Table 2.

Interpreting the WJ-III for English Language Proficiency

Oral Language RPI	CALPS Level	English Proficiency	Student will find related Level English language Tasks At Age or Grade Level
96/90 to 99/90	4.5 – 5	Average to Advanced	Very Easy to Manageable
82/90 to 95/90	4	Average	Manageable
68/90 to 95/90	3.5	Limited to Average	Manageable to Difficult
34/90 to 67/90	3	Limited	Difficult
19/90 to 33/90	2.5	Very Limited to Limited	Difficult to Extremely Difficult
5/90 to 18/90	2	Very Limited	Extremely Difficult
3/90 to 4/90	1.5	Negligible to Very Limited	Extremely Difficult to Impossible
0/90 to 2/90	1	Negligible	Impossible

Adapted from Hebert (2005)

Safeguards for ensuring appropriate identification of diverse learners

Salvia and Ysseldyke (2004) define assessment as the "process of collecting data for the purpose of making decisions about individuals and groups" (p 4). Although the assessment process of all students has proven a difficult task, culturally and linguistically diverse learners present unique challenges. Education professionals must become aware of students' cultural, linguistic, and experiential background, level of acculturation, sociolinguistic development, and cognitive learning styles. Such knowledge base is critical in developing a valid picture of the student and his/her capabilities and achievement levels. This information is vital for effective education decision-making.

Traditionally, intelligence tests have been administered to determine student eligibility for special education services, continuing a controversial practice (Herr & Bateman, 2003; Ysseldyke, 2005). The use of intelligence tests with individuals from diverse cultural and linguistic backgrounds is complex, and many practitioners have limited training in the selection and interpretation of tests when evaluating those with languages other than their own (Ortiz & Ochoa, 2005). Many students of color and who are linguistically diverse may be inappropriately identified, labeled, and placed in special education programs because of lack of comprehensive assessment practices that are insensitive to students' culture, language, and behavior patterns (Obiakor, Algozzine, Thurlow, Ogisi, Enwefa, Enwefa, & McIntosh, 2002). When evaluating students from linguistically and culturally diverse backgrounds, evaluation personnel must recognize that one size does not fit all (Warner, Dede, Garvan, & Conway, 2002).

Fair and equitable testing practices start with the acknowledgement that all tests of cognitive ability and intelligence are manifestations of the philosophy held by those who created them. Performance on these tests is an indication of how well the student being assessed has gained knowledge or learned skills and abilities that are deemed important by the culture. By recognizing the potential cultural and linguistic bias of specific tests, the examiner can begin to understand why an individual from a different culture may not perform as expected (Ortiz & Dynda, 2005). Very simply put, "their culture may not share the same knowledge or skills being sampled by the test" (Ortiz & Dynda, 2005, p. 547). Further, intelligence tests should not be used as a pure measure of aptitude or ability. Instead, they more appropriately would be viewed as indicators of achievement and part of an overall evaluation approach. If culturally and linguistically diverse students obtain low scores, it may mean that educational settings and instructional practices need revision (Sattler, 2001).

In order to ensure appropriate eligibility decisions are made for diverse students, assessors and educational personnel should utilize the Oral Language RPI and CALP scores to inform the decision making process. Such scores can provide pertinent information regarding a student's performance levels in language acquisition in relation to same age and grade peers. Additionally, through the interpretation of such scores, assessment professionals can better determine whether a student's academic deficits are due to insufficient language acquisition or a true disability. Furthermore, CALP levels should also be considered when planning instruction for diverse learners.

INTERCULTURAL UNDERSTANDING

Fostering the development of BICS and CALP for ELLs, including those with learning disabilities

Educational and cultural considerations must be taken into account when applying the theory of BICS and CALP to classroom instruction for language minority children. These considerations should not be exclusively limited to the classroom, but should be implemented and reflected schoolwide. Perhaps the single most important concern is the schoolwide acceptance of a pedagogy that places value on the linguistic and cultural experiences that children bring with them to the classroom. A pedagogy that places value on prior experiences is "responsive" to the needs and the abilities of the learner. The promotion and acceptance of such pedagogy is based upon the understanding that knowledge about language, culture, and human values is constructed in the home and community environments and that children's development and learning is best understood as the interaction of past and present experiences and knowledge (García, 2001). Also, according to García (2001), educators, administrators, and diagnosticians alike must adopt the belief that learning occurs best when it is embedded in a context that is socioculturally, linguistically, and cognitively relevant for the child. A pedagogy that respects and values a student's prior knowledge, including prior linguistic knowledge, will effectively assist the student in cognitive development in the second language.

As with culture, language is developed via family systems and the community. Language is a developmental process that usually begins at birth, is sequential, and builds upon itself (Ortiz & Dynda, 2005). In most cases, language is the primary means for establishing and negotiating meaning. It is intertwined with all prior communicative experiences and should therefore be accepted and utilized as a valid and valuable tool to promote the further development of the target language.

Expanding the theory of BICS and CALP to classroom instruction is based on the fundamental premise that students with limited English proficiency must first reach a "threshold" of native-language skills. Reaching the threshold of native-language proficiency in all domains, including listening, reading, writing and speaking, will equip the child with the language skills required to complete academic tasks with success and will promote the development of similar language-proficiency in English (Crawford, 1999). Cummins defines the threshold of native language proficiency as the level of linguistic competence that is sufficient to assist students in continuing their academic development. A child must obtain an adequate level of linguistic competence in his/her native language (L1) before a higher level of linguistic proficiency can be achieved in either the native language (L1) or the target language (L2) (MacSwan & Rolstad, 2005). Cummins maintains that children who are unable to reach the threshold level of development in the first language are likely to struggle academically in both languages (Crawford, 1999). What conditions/benchmarks must be present to reach the threshold level? If appropriately implemented, the following principles and their practical implications form the pedagogical framework needed to obtain native-language proficiency (threshold level):

- The development of proficiencies in both the native language and English has a positive effect on academic achievement for bilingual students;
- Language proficiency is defined as the ability to use language for basic communicative tasks and academic purposes;

- For ELLs, reaching the "threshold" of native-language skills is "key" to developing similar proficiency skills in English;
- Comprehensible second-language instruction and a supportive environment provide the supports needed for the acquisition of basic communicative competency in a second language; and
- The perceived status of students affects the interaction among all members of the educational setting and thus effects student outcomes (Crawford, 1999).

Selected practical instructional implications for such a pedagogy include the following:
- Instruction is provided in and through the native language;
- Initial reading classes and subjects requiring higher cognitive demands are taught in the native language;
- Students are provided with sufficient access to texts and supplementary materials in the native language;
- Instruction is provided by well-trained teachers with high levels of native-language proficiency; and
- Instruction is provided in the native language whenever possible rather than in a combination of the native language and English (Crawford, 1999).

Conclusion

The inability to perform targeted academic tasks and the inability to acquire academic language will greatly increase the chances of the child being placed at risk. As a result, the child may be inappropriately identified as having learning disabilities when in fact he/she is not. In this case, the deficits would be the direct result of an inability to acquire the academic language needed to perform the academic tasks with proficiency rather than a disorder in a basic psychological process. This paper was written to assist teachers in understanding the differences between the two types of language, BICS and CALP. It is especially essential that instruction for initial reading classes and other cognitively demanding subjects be taught in the child's native language (Crawford, 1999). As the content becomes more complex, so does the need for a vocabulary in both languages that is more cognitively demanding and academically specific in nature.

Reaching the threshold level of native language proficiency in both BICS and CALP is key to achieving grade-level academic proficiencies in the target language. Acquiring the academic language skills that are necessary for success is highly dependent upon the quality of the language development program and the length of time the students are allowed to participate. Experts maintain that language-minority children need at least five to seven years in an appropriately implemented bilingual/dual language program to develop the academic language skills needed to perform academic tasks at grade level and above (Crawford, 1999). Finally, as the diversity of our school populations continues to change, it is of paramount importance for school administrators, educators, and assessment personnel to be well trained in suitable assessment procedures and educational pedagogy for meeting the needs of all students.

References

Anderson, R. (1997). *The prevention of language disadvantage during second language acquisition of the child.* Retrieved December 19, 2006, from http://Home.earthlink.net/-psychron/prevent.

Anderson, R. (2004). *Outline of the assessment process: An outline of the assessment of the child during second language acquisition.* Retrieved January 3, 2007, from http://Home.earthlink.net/-ychron/outline.htm.

Crawford, J. (1999). *Bilingual education: History, politics, theory, and practice* (4th ed.). Los Angeles: Bilingual Educational Services, Inc.

Cummins, J. (1984). *Bilingualism and special education: Issues in assessment and pedagogy.* Clevedon, England: Multilingual Matters.

Cummins, J. (1989). *Empowering minority students.* Sacramento, CA: California Association for Bilingual Education.

Cummins, J. (2006). *Putting language proficiency in its place: Responding to critiques of the conversational/academic language distinction.* Retrieved on December 19, 2006, from http://www.iteachilearn.com/cummins/converacademlangdisti.html

Fuller, D. P., Miller, K. J., & Dominguez, L. (2006). Impact of a cultural self-analysis project: Increasing early childhood preservice teacher's cultural competency. *Multiple Voices, 9* (1), 12-21.

Garcia, E. (2001). *Hispanics education in the United States: Raices y alas.* Lanham, MD: Rowman & Littlefield.

Hebert, H. (2005). *Interpreting the WJ-III for English language proficiency.* Retrieved January 12, 2007, from http://www.upcd.org.

Herr, C.M., & Bateman, B. D. (2003). Learning disabilities and the law. In H. L. Swanson, K. R. Harris, & S. Graham (Eds), *Handbook of learning disabilities* (pp. 57-73). New York: Gilliford Press.

Klinger, J. K., & Artiles, A. J. (2003). When should bilingual students be in special education? *Educational Leadership, 61*(2), 66-71.

Lamb, G. D., Ochoa, S. H., & Garcia De Alba, R. (2006). Issues and interventions influencing the academic outcomes for migrant students. *Multiple Voices, 9*(1), 135-148.

Livingston, A., & Wirt, J. (2005). *The condition of education 2005 in brief (NCES Report No. 2005.095).* Washington, DC: U.S. Department of Education, National Center for Educational Statistics.

Loe, S.A., & Miranda, A. H. (2002). Assessment of culturally and linguistically diverse learners with behavioral disorders. In L. M. Bullock & A. Gable (Eds.), *Culturally and linguistically diverse students with behavior disorders* (pp. 25-36). Arlington, VA: Council for Exceptional Children.

MacSwan, J., & Rolstad, K. (2005). Modularity and the facilitation effect: Psychological mechanisms of transfer in bilingual students. *Hispanic Journal of Behavioral Sciences, 27*(2), 226.

Mercer, C. D., & Mercer, A. R. (1998). *Teaching students with learning problems* (5th ed.). Upper Saddle River, N J: Prentice Hall.

Obiakor, F., Algozzine, B., Thurlow, M., Gwalla-Ogis, N., Enwefa, S., Enwefa, R., & McIntosh, A. (2002). Addressing the issues of disproportionate representation. In L. Bullock & R.A. Gable (Eds.), *Culturally and linguistically diverse students with behavior disorders.* (1-9). Arlington, VA: Council for Exceptional Children.

Ortiz, A. A., & Yates, J. (1983). Incidence of exceptionality among Hispanics: Implications for manpower planning. *NABE Journal, 7,* 41-54.

Ortiz, S., & Dynda, A. (2005). Use of intelligence tests with culturally and linguistically diverse populations. In D. P. Flanagan & P.L. Harrison (Eds.), *Contemporary intellectual assessment: Theories and issues* (pp. 545-556). New York: The Guilford Press.

Ortiz, S., & Ochoa, S. H. (2005). Advances in cognitive assessment of culturally and linguistically diverse individuals: A nondiscriminatory interpretive approach. In D. P. Flanagan & P. L. Harrison (Eds.), *Contemporary intellectual assessment: Theories and issues* (pp. 234-250). New York: The Guilford Press.

Rhodes, R., Ochoa, S. H., & Ortiz, S. O. (2005). *Comprehensive assessment of culturally and linguistically diverse students: A practical approach.* New York: The Guilford Press.

Riverside Publishing. (2007, January 12). *Interpretation of Woodcock-Johnson III Tests.* Retrieved January 12, 2007, from http://www.riverpub.com.

Rosberry-McKibbin, C. (2007). *Language disorders in children* (pp. 67-101). Boston: Pearson Education.

Salvia, J., & Ysseldyke, J. (2004). *Assessment in special and inclusive education* (9th ed.) Boston: Houghton Mifflin.

Santos, R. M., Corso, R. M., & Maude, S. (2006). Meaningful participation of diverse constituents: The culturally and linguistically appropriate service institute. *Multiple Voices, 9*(1), 34-49.

Sattler, J. M., & Dumont, R. (2004). *Assessment of children: WISC-IV and WPPSI-III supplement* (pp. 1-56). La Mesa, CA: Jerome M. Sattler Press.

Sattler, J. M. (2001). *Assessment of children: Cognitive supplement* (4th ed.). La Mesa, CA: Jerome M. Sattler Press.

Texas Education Agency (2004-2005). *Academic excellence indicator system.* Retrieved April 10, 2007, from http://www.tea.state.tx.us/perfreport/aeis/2005/state.html.

Warner, T. D., Dede, D. E., Garvan, C. W., & Conway, T. W. (2002). One size still does not fit all in specific learning disability assessment across ethnic groups. *Journal of Learning Disabilities, 35*(6), 500-508.

Ysseldyke, J. (2005). Assessment and decision making for students with learning disabilities: What if this is as good as it gets? *Learning Disability Quarterly, 28,* 125-128.

Contemplating Community through Multicultural Children's Literature

Janelle Mathis
University of North Texas

Multicultural children's literature is well established as a resource for culturally responsive and culturally relevant classrooms. Over twenty-five years beyond Rudine Sims Bishop's (1982) analogy of literature being a mirror and a window for children to see themselves and view others, multicultural literature has assumed a variety of responsibilities across the curriculum, most recently including teaching critical literacy and thinking (Lewison, Flint, & Van Sluys, 2002; McDaniel, 2004); nurturing multicultural insights and perspectives (Dressel, 2005; Fox & Short, 2003; Louie, 2006); finding one's own identity (Blackford, 2004; Dutro, 2003), using literacy for empowerment (Damico, 2005); and teaching about social justice (Damico & Riddle, 2004; Wolk, 2004) and democracy (Ching, 2005). As our society becomes increasingly diverse, these various functions of children's and adolescent literature represent critical points of inquiry and discussion for both teachers and students.

Supporting these important responsibilities is an ever-increasing abundance of literature that focuses on a variety of contemporary themes as well as brings new light to historical issues. A recent analysis of numerous themes in studies regarding children's literature revealed an interesting strand that consistently emerged across the topics as a function of children's literature in the classroom—that of creating community and positioning readers to realize their role in building, supporting, and belonging to community. Establishing a sense of community within the classroom as well as nurturing a sense of the local and global communities is an ongoing goal of classroom teachers (O'Brien, 2001; Short, Harste, with Burke, 1996; Van Horn, 2001). Additionally, those concerned with issues of diversity to include ethnicity, gender or the global community (Dutro, Kazemi, & Balf, 2005; Smith, 2005) address the role of these communities in the lives of its members. Literature is often used to teach about these various communities and to help readers make personal connections to various social groups. However, community membership requires a variety of factors that determine how individuals' perceptions of themselves, the community, and their involvement in a particular group help them position their membership in that community. Therefore, the theme of "community" has been chosen here as a way to explore one approach to choosing and using multicultural literature—through multicultural text sets. Suggested titles for other themes related to community are included as well. It is the hope that individuals reading this will realize that the possibilities of multicultural literature lie within their own willingness to read and respond to these titles. Teachers can explore and learn through the rich insights in children's literature with their students, since many teachers come from educational backgrounds that did not value the possibilities of individual cultural capital that each student brings to the learning situation.

Besides a basis in the various theories of culturally responsive teaching and the various areas of research in multicultural literature mentioned above, the ideas here are also based in sociocultural perspectives of literacy (Street, 1984). Multicultural literature's use in classrooms is described here in ways that go beyond decoding and comprehension of the written text to thinking and acting in ways that ultimately shape the readers' social existence. Additionally, the identity aspect of the work of James Gee who speaks of Discourse and refers to "ways of being in the world or forms of life which integrate words, acts, values, beliefs, attitudes, and social identities . . ." (1996, p. 127) and the insights of Fairclough on social change (1992) provides support for the complex possibilities of the role of children's literature in classrooms.

Defining a text set

The organizational strategy of creating and using a text set is the framework around which multicultural titles are introduced here. A text set is five to fifteen texts that relate conceptually in some way, such as similar themes, topics, and other organizing concepts (Short, Harste, with Burke, 1996). A text set should reflect different perspectives on a particular theme or concept and a multicultural text set places importance on the diversity of people and cultures that present varied perspectives on a given topic. As a teacher or student creates a text set, he / she considers a variety of criteria, such as genre (defined quite broadly and inclusive of non-print resources); knowledge systems (ways of perceiving the world through the lens of different paradigms of thought, such as history, ecology, politics, and social sciences); cultural representation; a range of reading levels of books; and criteria specific to the particular topic under consideration. Besides a variety of frames for discussion and response following reading the books, engagements that extend the insights gained from the text set are planned that involve writing, drama, music, art, and other sign systems as well as further discussion that might purposefully build on intertextual potential (Mathis, 2002).

INTERCULTURAL UNDERSTANDING

A text set is created by first reading extensively and making notes, perhaps on an inquiry chart, to record the various perspectives for each title read. Then, selecting the set from this extensive reading requires intensive contemplation of the various titles. As the person creating the text set reads, the framing focus or question narrows and a more refined purpose frames the discussions and strategies. For example, if the set is on community, perhaps the guiding question is

- What are the components of community? or,
- Who are the people who make up a community and how do they support each other? or,
- What types of communities do individuals participate in and how does the participation help shape who we are?

The many books read are then considered in light of the perspective that is presented.

Criteria for excellence in multicultural literature for children

Of course, of critical importance in selecting these books are the criteria that speak to authenticity, accuracy, and objectivity in children's literature. A more in depth discussion of these criteria may be found (Fox & Short, 2003; Norton, 2006; Vandergrift, 2006) and include such factors as:

- characters are portrayed accurately and uniquely rather than stereotypically;
- the culture is naturally portrayed within the context of the story;
- illustrations accurately show people and situations;
- historical information is researched and used accurately.

However, Ching (2005) has poignantly reminded educators that to only look at these tangible traits, while they "offer crucial support for intercultural awareness," one may overlook "deeper ideologies that affect the distribution of power in society" (p. 129). As educators prepare to teach children within a culturally responsive classroom, they must develop and promote cultural sensitivity and awareness for themselves as well as their children. In doing so, they cannot disregard books that address the intersection of culture, race and power and how "issues of power in intercultural contexts" (Ching, p. 129) provide an important aspect of multicultural literature to consider. For many teachers, such considerations may be new, but books that point to issues of equity and inequity are necessary as readers consider a democratic community. Authenticity in children's literature must include, or at least invite, these discussions around power, race, and culture. Fox and Short (2003) point to issues that raise debates around "the power to narrate, the power to tell one's own story, the power to self-determine, the power to self-realize, the power to self-represent, the power to change inequity into equity, the power to articulate reparation for historical injustice" (Ching, p. 129). For these reasons, the books selected here are inclusive of titles that reflect issues of power as well as books that celebrate the pluralism and universalities that bring people together.

A multicultural text set on community

Although creating community is often a desired outcome of classroom instructional strategies, ways to achieve this sense of community are often addressed at merely a surface level. Various components work toward inviting individuals to be part of any community—the context in place, personal issues and perceptions of self, perceptions of the various communities, investment in communities through active involvement to bring about change or improvement. As research in children's literature offers many perspectives through which to view instruction, this literature can also speak to a complexity of factors that affect how a reader perceives his/her own involvement in a community. The discussion here begins with a familiar book—*Seedfolks* (Fleischman, 1997). Many readers are familiar with this collection of 13 vignettes, told from first person, and woven together into a larger story of how a vacant, trashed lot in an inner city neighborhood became a community garden. Begun by a young Vietnamese girl paying respect and connecting to the dead father she never knew by planting lima beans, the garden is created into a community for members whose needs and purposes for joining are as numerous as there are gardeners. Author Paul Fleischman, a skilled artisan at creating story from multiple voices, tells the story of this unique place where 13 individuals connect—young and old, some immigrants but all diverse in their life experiences. Each finds within the garden a community where his/her voice is heard and where he/she can interact with others. Each brings a unique contribution to the garden and each is hopeful of a variety of outcomes for different reasons. Each is supported in interesting ways by others as they interact and learn of each other and themselves.

Upon reading this, most can agree that it has implications for how and for what purpose a community is created, and while not an entity in itself for defining "community," it can well serve as an initial point to begin extensive reading and selecting other books to widen the notion of community building for young readers. While this particular book is most relevant to upper elementary, middle school and beyond, it offers themes for the present discussion that can draw from both picture and chapter books and, thus, provide possibilities for texts for both younger and older readers with the addition of other books selected for the appropriate levels. As mentioned earlier, it is through the reading and personal response of the teacher that books become powerful instruments to help readers connect to a particular theme. The teacher's connections as learner are important here as is the willingness to learn of any community leader. As a teacher reads extensively, he/she will determine the best books for his/her class based on their needs and the criteria described earlier.

As described above, *Seedfolks* provides a microcosmic parallel as to how a diverse society might come to be and ultimately thrive because of their shared commitment to the larger goal—in this case, creating a garden. Of course, as mentioned, the garden has different purposes for different people. For example, Sae Young is from Korea and the garden helps her overcome her fear of people and her loneliness after the death of her husband. Over time she is able to say the individuals there are "almost like family." Gonzalo's Tio Juan was well respected in his former home; however, unable to speak to anyone in the U.S., the garden restores his self-respect since his expertise in gardening is highly regarded without speaking English. Amir feels the garden's benefit was "to make the eyes see our neighbors" (Fleischman, 1997, p. 59). It was an escape from the isolation he found when coming to America. Conversations tied those in the garden together and transformed relationships. Curtis, always a favorite of readers, was a ladies' man with large muscles and an over-inflated self-concept. The garden was his hope to show his commitment and rebuild a relationship with the only person he loved.

Since the characters here found strength, identity, and purpose in the garden community, extensive reading offered many potential

INTERCULTURAL UNDERSTANDING

books that spoke to the significant role of community in the lives of diverse people as they both gave and received from others. The following books represent one potential text set as they present multiple perspectives across genre, cultures, the type and purpose of the community, and ultimately how it was established. Each perspective is important and each book offers a unique contribution to the set. This text set on community, to include *Seedfolks*, points to diverse cultural groups and points to universal needs across cultures to which many diverse readers in a classroom can connect.

Dear Mr. Rosenwald (Weatherford, 2006) tells of a small southern African American community in the early years of the 20th century, which, in an effort to create a school for its children, provides an inspiring example of a community working together for a common purpose. Members of the community hear of an offer by Julius Rosenwald, the president of Sears, Roebuck, and Co., to fund the building of schools for communities willing to provide additional funds and they successfully accept this challenge.

¡Sí, Se Puede!, Yes, We Can! (Cohn, 2002) shares another community endeavor—the janitor strike in Los Angeles in 2000 for better wages. The people in this group, to include the children, worked together to peacefully increase their respect and salaries. This book maintains integrity but is told simply in order for young readers to realize why the strike occurred and how children were affected.

A Sweet Smell of Roses (Johnson, 2005) tells of the earlier civil rights movement from the perspective of a child and pays tribute to the children who marched for freedom. Many books exist that point to the communities that participated in the larger effort for equality, and the child's perspective of this one makes it quite useful for children to consider their role in a community's activities. The sweet smell of freedom is a prize for all ages.

Additionally, for older readers, *Freedom Walkers: The Story of the Montgomery Bus Boycott* (Freedman, 2006) provides a community determined to find justice and freedom despite life-threatening and stressful situations. The African American community of Montgomery, Alabama, is a prime example of community members displaying strength, identity, and purpose. This inspiring story of the beginning of the civil rights movement is shared through individual stories of the people who belonged to this community.

Shared cultural traditions and daily life events are highlighted in a story about an African community in Mali, *I Lost My Tooth in Africa* (Diakité, 2006). When a little girl loses her tooth, this seemingly universal event provides points for diverse discussion as she receives a chicken from the tooth fairy. This delightful tale is also full of authentic insights of the village where the author's extended family live.

A Place Where Sunflowers Grow (Lee-Tai & Lee, 2006) shares a community where the members depend on each other for hope and reassurance in a time of harsh injustice. The Japanese internment camps during World War II found people working together as communities despite the conditions and political mind set that brought them together. This is one of several accounts that point to the supporting nature of these communities. In this story a little girl finds hope in friends, art, and growing sunflowers.

An earlier book that was created for older readers, *Children of Topaz: The Story of a Japanese American Internment Camp* (Tunnel & Chilcoat, 1996), uses a focus on a school in Topaz to provide a powerful description of life in an internment community. The author's research gives voice and integrity to the individuals involved and points to their continued participation in society as active community members after they were released from the camps.

A charming imagined community awaits the reader of *Porch Lies: Tales of Slicksters, Tricksters, and Other Wily Characters* (McKissack, 2006). The variety of characters in this collection speak to the communities from which they come and the oral tradition that prevailed. As each character uniquely contributes in good or not-so-good ways, the potential reality of this community is made obvious by the author's vocabulary, detail, and familiar humorous character traits.

Communities work to support the individuals therein, but they also must learn about other cultural groups/communities in efforts to live peacefully. *Henry and the Kite Dragon* (Hall, 2004) looks at two distinct groups of children, Chinese and Italian, living in New York City in the 1920s. They learn to make space for the cultural traditions of each after discovering that their ongoing conflict could be resolved by understanding and acknowledging the daily lives and needs of each group.

A community might exist across time, such as the community of jazz musicians, singers, and enthusiasts. *Jazz* (Meyers, 2006) is a collection of 15 poems that speak to the senses about this rich cultural community and their contribution to all of society through its various members. Additionally, *Rent Party Jazz* (Miller, 2001) provides a more focused look at one community in New Orleans in which a traditional, informal fund-raising jazz benefit brings a community together to support one of its members in need while enjoying the music of a local trumpet player. Sharing traditions, problem solving, and supporting its own are all community characteristics found in this book.

INTERCULTURAL UNDERSTANDING

Here in Harlem, also by Meyers (2006) also captures for older students the unique voices of the same era as Jazz, but focuses this well known community in New York City. In 54 free verse poems, Meyers captures the joys, sorrows, dreams, arts, history, and unique personalities that make up this well-known community. Through these individual voices the reader is invited into this culturally rich community and realizes that it is the individual lives that make the rich fabric of a community.

The Cat with the Yellow Star: Coming of Age in Terezin (Rubin & Weissberger, 2006) is but one example of the communities established during World War II due to the Holocaust. In 1942 Ella Weissberger became a member of a concentration camp in Terezin, Czechoslovakia. Amidst the horrific, fearful, circumstances that brought these people together, they organized around and focused on creative endeavors under the guidance of artists and musicians to maintain a semblance of the life they once knew. The hopeful, supportive nature of a community is at its most powerful in many of the Holocaust narratives for children.

Cooperation within and between communities often serve to make the world a better place. *Crossing Bok Chitto* (Tingle, 2006) is the story of a Choctaw girl and slave boy helping a slave family escape hunters points to the greater community of mankind to which all belong. While numerous stories of the underground railway might also provide a choice of books to add to this set, the unique role of support from very diverse groups here is a valuable insight for students.

Going farther back in history, *Malian's Song* (Bruchac, 2006), tells of the attack on an Abenaki community in 1759 by the English—an attack that was recorded in British journals at the time as destroying everyone. However, through the oral tradition, stories of this battle have been passed down and collected and pointed to the number of survivors dispersed throughout the area. This narrative speaks to the strength and fortitude of a community and to the role of story to maintain its rich history.

Strategies to help readers connect to their own communities

As with any book or set of books, the potential power of literature is limited by the ways in which it is used. A context that invites and values personal response is one in which the notion of community is already in process. As students respond personally, question, and discuss the responses of others, they learn about the life experiences that each brings to the classroom. As this dialogue points to connections often between the local community or various cultural communities of which students are a part, these insights become a foundation for which understanding is built. As one character said in *Seedfolks* when asked by a shop owner why she had treated him as she had in the past, "Back then, I didn't know it was you" (Fleischman, 1997, p. 64). We want our students to know each other just as we hope to know the cultures and communities from which they come. It is only when we can weave together the threads from their various individual communities that a new tapestry depicting the classroom community is formed—a tapestry that tells stories from the lives of all its members.

In addition to discussion, participatory extension activities can provide ways for students to use their cultural backgrounds as they engage in considering characters and contexts through writing, music, art, and drama. Such instructional strategies should always be ones that invite students to begin with their own life experiences as they connect to the books they are exploring and as they connect to the lives of other students as revealed through the various responses to text. Learning is socially constructed (Vygotsky, 1986) and the process of learning in culturally responsive contexts reciprocally builds the social contexts—the community— for further learning. Just as the books in the text set speak to strength, mutual support, identity, voice, and purpose in community, so the discussions and strategies around such titles have the potential to nurture the development of these criteria within the classroom.

The most appropriate student activities that might be used to extend thinking around the theme of a particular text set are directly linked to the unique communities to which students belong. In addition, several general ideas that can be adapted are:

- Brainstorm and web the characteristics of a community as found in responses to these books. Then, discuss how these characteristics might be part of the classroom community. Create a collage or mural that depicts these characteristics.

- Ask each student to consider the community or neighborhood of which they are a part. Discuss ways they support each other and work towards a common purpose using examples from the books they have read. Is there an issue that currently needs decisions or action within the local community? How is it or how might it be resolved? How might the student be involved? Listen to the local news for evidence of how communities work together to resolve problems. Record these for later reflection.

- Ask students to pick someone from their local community that they feel contributes significantly to the community. Write about that person and create a class book that points to the contributions of each.

INTERCULTURAL UNDERSTANDING

- Process drama entails tableau, enactments, positioning oneself within the text or creating a scene that could have been part of the text. It often invites readers to become part of the story. These forms of engagement can be especially powerful as young readers put themselves in the shoes of others and consider the actions, decisions, and emotional situations that many individuals face. Some possible process drama approaches to this text set might be: (1) Ask readers in groups to create a scene from a book of their choice in which the community is working or celebrating together. Others can guess the scene and book noting how the positions and facial expressions help to relate the experience portrayed in the scene. (2) Create a panel of characters who were rendered voiceless or powerless in situations within the text set, and yet they proved to be resilient. Let students decide questions they would like to ask these people and conduct an interview with the students portraying these individuals. Those being interviewed will have to be "in role" and create answers based on what they have learned from their reading.

- Write from the perspective of someone in one of the communities, such as in a community struggling for freedom or in the garden community in *Seedfolks*. For example, envision yourself as a person in the Cleveland neighborhood where *Seedfolks* took place. Write a first person narrative following the style of Fleischman. You can be someone who decides to join the gardeners or someone who is observing them. The response connections that each writer shares here also point to their assuming a position in this community. This might be a follow-up point for discussion.

- Ask readers to identify an important quote from each book. From these, pick one that might be used as a repetitive line that summarizes a major theme that readers found within the various communities in the books. Arrange the quotations, alternating with the repetitive line, into a choral reading to perform with multiple voices.
- Hold a story telling festival in which each student tells a story from his cultural community. This can be an old "yarn" that is told frequently and shared within a cultural group or it might be a story about an event that happened in one's neighborhood or town. Encourage students to create images through the senses as they tell the stories so others can visualize the situation or character they are describing.
- Many poetry forms are currently used to invite students to share through sensory imagery their own backgrounds. For example, the "Where I'm From Poem" (found in numerous websites framed after a poem by George Ella Lyon and also in Van Horn, 2001) offers a wonderful framework for each student to describe his/her own community. The poems of Walter Dean Meyers in *Harlem Stomp!* provide another poetic format to use as a model. Several interesting models for writing poetry across the curriculum are found in Sara Holbrook's *Practical Poetry* (2005), and for community ideas, in particularly, in the section on social studies. Her poetry begins with the rich experiences students bring to the classroom, and such strategies as "It's Not Fair" ask young writers to take both sides of the story as does her poem "Fortunately. . . Unfortunately."

INTERCULTURAL UNDERSTANDING

- Ask students to read international news via newspapers or the Internet or listen to international news reports. In a double entry journal, write on one side, what is being reported. In the other column, write what information is missing in order to understand the situation in the news report? Why is further insight necessary to understand the situation, the decisions being made, or the perspectives shared? Draw parallels between this and their classroom community as well as reference *Henry and the Kite Dragon*. Discuss how it is important to plan around everyone's needs.

Conclusion

In addition to suggested titles around a theme of community, other themes that are directly related to this concept are provided here. These potential titles for multicultural text sets, inclusive of both picture and chapter books, offer beginning points for critical discussions in classrooms and invite the addition of other texts and non-print resources, such as music or art. Teachers are encouraged to continually seek other titles that fit their own interpretation of these and other themes—titles that enrich understandings of other cultures as well as give voice to diverse people both within and outside one's own community.

A sampling of other sets

Sense of place

Bruchac, Joseph. (1999). *Between Earth and Sky: Legends of Native American Sacred Places.* Illustrated by Thomas Locker. New York: Harcourt.

INTERCULTURAL UNDERSTANDING

Coburn, Jewell Reinhart. *Angkat, The Cambodian Cinderella.* Illustrated by Eddie Flotte. Auburn, CA: Shen's Books.

Halilbegovich, Nadja. (2006). *My Childhood Under Fire: A Sarajevo Diary.* Tonawanda, NY: Kids Can Press.

Hill, Laban Corrick. *Harlem Stomp!* A Cultural history of the Harlem Renaissance. Illustrated by Megen Tingley. New York: Little Brown.

Lendroth, Susan. *Why Explore?* Illustrated by Enrique S. Moreiro. Berkeley, CA: Tricycle Press.

Nye, Naomi. (2002). *100 Varieties of Gazelles.* New York: Greenwillow.

McKissack, Patricia. (2002). *Goin' Someplace Special.* Illustrated by Jerry Pinkney. New York: Atheneum.

Ruurs, Margriet. (2005). *My Librarian is a Camel.* Honesdale, PA: Boyds Mills Press.

Stroud, Bettye. (2005). *The Patchwork Path: A Quilt Map to Freedom.* Illustrated by Erin Susanne Bennett. New York: Candlewick.

Tunnell, Michael & Chilcoat, George W. (1995). *Children of Topaz: the Story of a Japanese Internment Camp.* New York: Holiday House.

Seeking identity

Carvel, Marlene. (2005). *SweetGrass Basket.* New York: Penguin.

Grimes, Nikki. *Bronx Masquerade.* New York: Dial/Penguin Putnam.

Kyuchukov, Hirsto. (2004). *My Name Was Hussein.* Illustrated by Allan Eitzen. Honesdale, PA: Boyds Mills Press.

Lester, Julius (2005). *Lets Talk about Race.* Illustrated by Karen Barbour. New York: Harper Collins.

INTERCULTURAL UNDERSTANDING

Reich, Susanna. (2005). *Jose! Born to Dance: The Story of Jose Limon*. Illustrated by Raul Colon. New York: Simon & Schuster.

Rembert, Winferd. (2004). *Don't Hold Me Back: My Life and Art*. New York: Cricket.

Ryan, Pam Munoz. (2005). *Becoming Naomi Leon*. New York: Scholastic.

Singer, Marilyn, ed. (2005). *Face Relations: 11 Stories about Seeing Beyond Color*. New York: Simon & Schuster.

Wong, Janet. (2002). *Apple Pie, Fourth of July*. Illustrated by Margaret Chodos-Irvine. New York: Harcourt.

Woodson, Jacquelin. (2005). *Show Way*. Illustrated by Hudson Talbott. New York: G. P. Putnam's Sons.

Immigrants: Resiliency before and after

Ahmedi, Farah. (2005). *The Story of My Life, An Afghan Girl on the Other Side of the Sky*. New York: Simon & Schuster.

Bunting, Eve. (2006). *One Green Apple*, Illustrated by Ted Lewin. New York: Houghton Mifflin.

Gallo, Donald R. (2004). *First Crossing: Stories about Teen Immigrants*. Cambridge, MA: Candlewick.

Hoffman, M. (2002). *The Color of Home*. New York: Dial.

Jaramillo, Ann. (2006). *La linea*. New York: Roaring Brook.

Krinitz, Esther Nisenthal & Steinhardt, Bernice. (2005). *Memories of Survival*. New York: Hyperion.

Medina, Jane. (2004). *Dream on Blanca's Wall: Poems in English and Spanish*. Robert Casilla (Illustrator). Honesdale, PA: Boyds Mills Press.

Sachs, Marilyn. (2005). *Lost in America*. New Milford, CN: Roaring Brook Press.

Tal, Eve (2005). *Double Crossing.* El Paso, TX: Cinco Puntos Press.

Warren, Andrea. (2004). *Escape from Saigon, How a Vietnam War Orphan Became an American Boy.* New York: Farrar, Straus, Giroux.

Seeking a peaceful existence

Ellis, D. (2004). *Three wishes: Palestinian and Israeli Children Speak.* Berkeley, CA: Groundwood Books.

Gilley, Jeremy. (2005). *Peace One Day: The Making of World Peace Day.* Illustrated by Karen Blessen. New York: Putnam.

Greenfield, Eloise. (2006). *When the Horses Ride By: Children in the Times of War.* Illustrated by Jan Spivey Gilcrest. New York: Lee & Low.

Gottfried, Ted. (2005). *The Fight for Peace, A History of antiwar Movements in American.* Minneapolis: 21st Century Books.

Hall, Bruce Edward. (2004). *Henry and the Kite Dragon.* Illustrated by William Low. New York: Philomel.

Katz, Karen. (2006). *Can You Say Peace?* New York: Henry Holt.

McKee, David. (2004). *The Conquerors.* England: Handprint

McCutcheon, John (2006). *Christmas in the Trenches.* Illustrated by Henri Sorensen. Atlanta: Peachtree.

Vaugelade, Anais. (2001). The War. Translated by Marie-Christine Rouffiae and Tom Streissguth. First published in France. Carolrhoda.

Zalban, Jane Breckon. (2006). *Paths to Peace: People Who changed the World.* New York: Dutton.

INTERCULTURAL UNDERSTANDING

Children's books cited for community text set

Bruchac, Marge. (2006). *Malian's Song*. Illustrated by William Maugham. Middlebury, VT: Vermont Folk Life Center.

Diakité, Penda. (2006). *I Lost My Tooth in Africa*. Illustrated by Babe Wagué Diakité. New York: Scholastic.

Freedman, Russell. (2006). *Freedom Walkers: The Story of the Montgomery Bus Boycott*. New York: Holiday House.

Hall, Buce Edward. (2005). *Henry and the Kite Dragon*. Illusrated by William Low. New York: Philomel/Penguin.

Lee-Tai, Amy. (2006). *A Place Where Sunflowers Grow*. Illustrated by Felicia Hoshino. San Francisco: Children's Book Press.

McKissack, P. C. (2006). *Porch Lies: Tales of Slicksters, Tricksters, and Other Wily Characters*. Illustrated by André Carrilho. New York: Schwartz & Wade/Random House.

Myers, Walter Dean. (2006). *Jazz*. New York: Holiday House.

Myers, Walter Dean. (2004). *Here in Harlem*. New York: Holiday House.

Rubin, Susan Goldman & Weissberger, Ella. (2006). *The Cat with the Yellow Star: Coming of Age in Terezin*. New York: Holiday House.

Tingle, Tim. (2006). *Crossing Bok Chitto: A Choctaw Tale of Friendship & Freedom*. Illustrated by Jeanne Rorex Bridges. El Paso, TX: Cinco Puntos Press.

Tunnell, Michael & Chilcoat, George. (1996). *Children of Topaz: The Story of a Japanese American Internment Camp*. New York: Holiday House.

Weatherford, Carole Boston. *Dear Mr. Rosenwald.* Illustrated by R. Gregory Christie. New York: Scholastic.

References

Blackford, H. V. (2004). *Out of this world, why literature matters to girls.* New York: Teachers College Press.

Ching, S. H. D. (2005). Multicultural children's literature as an instrument of power. *Language Arts, 83,* 128-136.

Damico, J. S. (2005). Evoking hearts and heads: Exploring issues of social justice through poetry. *Language Arts, 83,* 137-146.

Damico, J. S., & Riddle, R. (2004). From answers to questions: A beginning teacher learns to teach for social justice. *Language Arts, 82,* 36-46.

Dressel, J. H. (2005). Personal response and social responsibility: Responses of middle school students to multicultural literature. *The Reading Teacher, 58,* 750-764.

Dutro, E. (2003). "Us boys like to read football and boy stuff": Reading masculinities, performing boyhood. *Journal of Literacy Research, 34,* 465-500.

Dutro, E., Kazemi, E., & Balf, R. (2005). The aftermath of "You're only half": Multiracial identities in the literacy classroom. *Language Arts, 83,* 96-106.

Fairclough, N. (1992). *Discourse and social change.* Cambridge, UK: Polity Press.

Fleischman, P. (1997). *Seedfolks.* New York: Harper Collins.

Fox, D. L., & Short, K. G. (2003). *Stories matter, the complexity of culturalauthenticity in children's literature.* Urbana, IL: NCTE.

Gee, J. P. (1996). *Social linguistics and literacies* (2nd Ed.). New York: Routledge Falmer.

Holbrook, S. (2005). *Practical poetry.* Portsmouth, NH: Heinemann.

Lewison, M., Flint, A., & Van Sluys, K. (2002). Taking on critical literacy: The journey of newcomers and novices. *Language Arts, 79,* 382-392.

Mathis, J. (2002). Multicultural text sets: Organizing for critical thinking. *The New Review of Children's Literature and Librarianship, 8,* 55-69.

McDaniel, C. (2004). Critical literacy: A questioning stance and the possibility for change. *Language Arts, 82,* 472-481.

Norton, D., & Norton, S. (2006). *Through the eyes of a child: An introduction to children's literature.* Boston: Pearson Education, Inc.

O'Brien, J. (2001). Children reading critically: A local history. In B. Comber & A. Simpson (Eds.), *Negotiating critical literacies in classrooms* (pp. 37-54). Mahwah, NJ: Lawrence Erlbaum.

Short, K., Harste, J. C. with Burke, C. (1996). *Creating classrooms for authors and inquirers,* (2nd ed.). Portsmouth, NH: Heinemann.

Sims-Bishop, R. (1982). *Shadow and substance.* Urbana, IL: National Council of Teachers of English.

Smith, S. (2005). "We feel like we're separating us": Sixth grade girls respond to multicultural literature. In B. Maloch, J. V. Hoffman, D. L. Schallert, C. M. Fairbanks, & J. Worthy, (Eds.), *Fifty-fourth yearbook of the national reading conference,* p.362-375. Oak Creek, WI: National Reading Conference.

Van Horn, L. (2001). *Creating literacy communities in the middle school.* Norwood, MA: Christopher-Gordon.

Vandergrift, K. (2006). Retrieved from http://www.scils.rutgers.edu/~kvander/ChildrenLit/

Vygotsky, L. (1986). *Thought and language.* Cambridge, MA: MIT Press.

Wenger, E. (1998). *Communities of practice: Learning, meaning, and identity.* Cambridge, UK: Cambridge University Press.

Wolk, S. (2004). Using picture books to teach for democracy. *Language Arts 82(1),* 26-35.

Creating an Inclusive Learning Community: Lessons from the Geese

**Joyce Rademacher
Karen Dunlap
Jane Pemberton
Texas Woman's University**

Ms. Rader is a fourth grade teacher in an urban school in Dallas, Texas. It is right before Thanksgiving and Ms. Rader reflects on the success of Jose, Maria, and Fernando, who are all English language learners (ELLs). She attributes their success to the instructional activities she implemented at the beginning of the year that included ideas from all of her students on how to create a predictable classroom environment. She knows that her students are able to focus on and enjoy learning when the classroom makes them feel comfortable. As a result, Jose, Maria, and Fernando enjoy working in cooperative groups with the assistance of their English proficient peers. Because her students know how to responsibly work together, Ms. Rader can plan activities that give ELLs more opportunities to participate in ways that are less demanding linguistically, but still require higher-order thinking skills. For example, Fernando was especially pleased with the pictorial record of the stages of a butterfly that he observed in science class. Other members of his group prepared written and oral documentation of the observations and presented it to the class. Ms. Rader also believes Jose, Maria, and Fernando have increased their speaking and writing vocabulary as a result of positive peer interactions. Yes, Ms. Rader is pleased that she took the time at the beginning of the year to engage students in creating a positive learning community where all students now feel connected to each other and to learning. The story she used, Lessons from the Geese, proved to be an excellent tool for teaching the concept of a learning community in a concrete way.

INTERCULTURAL UNDERSTANDING

As Ms. Rader discovered, much may be learned from the wisdom of the geese on how members of a community can help and support one another. As caring educators of diverse populations, we invite you to read and reflect on the following story as an example of how to create a classroom community with your students based on how geese create a community:

Lessons from the Geese

In the Fall, we can see geese heading south for the winter. Geese always fly along in V formation. This is what science has discovered about why geese fly that way:

As each bird flaps its wings, it creates an uplift for the bird right behind it.

By flying in V formation, the whole flock adds at least 71% greater flying range than if each bird flew on its own.

When one goose falls out of formation, it suddenly feels the drag and resistance of trying to fly alone. It quickly gets back into formation to take advantage of the lifting power of the bird in front.

When the head goose gets tired, it rotates back to another position in the wing. When that happens, another goose flies point.

Geese honk from behind and encourage those up front to keep up their speed.

Finally... and this is very important. When a goose gets sick or hurt, it falls out of formation. Two other geese then fall out with that hurt goose and follow it down to lend help and protection. They stay with the fallen goose until it is able to fly or until it dies. Only then do the two helping geese launch out on their own to catch up with the group. (McNeish, as cited in Rademacher, Pemberton, & Cheever, 2006a).

As you read the story, did you come to some conclusions about how geese function in their learning community? Did you also think about how to create a learning community with your students based on some of the same principles as the geese? Without these principles, Jose, Maria, and Fernando may not have experienced success. Figure 1 gives comparisons between how geese live in their community and how students may function in a learning community (Rademacher, et al. 2006a). See Figure 1.

Figure 1. Comparing Functions of Geese and Students in a Community

Geese and Students in a Community

Geese	Students
1. Have the same goal to get to a certain place.	1. Have the same goal to be good learners;
2. To do this, they fly in the same direction;	2. To do this, they study the same things;
3. Find it easier to fly in formation than alone;	3. Find it easier to work together than alone;
4. Don't bump into one another.	4. Don't bother other students as they work;
5. Do their individual jobs;	5. Create original work;
6. Help geese who are sick or hurt;	6. Help students who have trouble learning;

INTERCULTURAL UNDERSTANDING

7. Take turns leading; and/or	7. Take turns leading activities; and/or
8. Honk to encourage others to keep flying.	8. Encourage other students to keep trying and learning.

The purpose of this article is to share research on what educators can do to create classroom environments where *all* students can be taught to work together in a responsible, respectful, and safe manner. For this writing, *all* students refers to every learner in a classroom inclusive of cultural, linguistic and academic differences. First, the characteristics of inclusive learning communities will be discussed. Second, Positive Behavior Support (PBS) will be presented as a validated approach relevant for *all* students because it provides a supportive culture that encourages and supports students like Jose, Maria and Fernando. Third, a set of learning community expectations that is based on the principles of responsible work habits, respect and safety will be presented. Finally, instructional procedures on how to use "Lessons from the Geese" as an analogy for creating inclusive learning communities will be shared.

Characteristics of inclusive learning communities

Effective instruction for all students begins when teachers intentionally establish positive learning communities in which students learn to respect and value each other's differences. This is especially true for ELLs. To create such a learning community, teachers must help students understand their roles and responsibilities, show students how to work in a self-directed manner, and enlist student participation in setting classroom expectations for learning and getting along with others (Turnbull, Turnbull, & Wehmeyer, 2007).

According to Vernon, Schumaker, and Deshler (2000), the need for learning communities has never been greater because students come from a variety of cultures, racial/ethnic backgrounds, and religions. As a result, these students bring to the classroom a variety of experiences and different ways of viewing the world around them. They also exhibit a wide range of academic and social skills. Vernon et al. (2000), further state that in spite of such diverse characteristics, students need to feel "connected" to both education and the school in order to experience success. In fact, the major goal of any learning community is to help students make just such a connection. However, for students like Jose, Maria, and Fernando, whose level of understanding and capabilities reside in a language other than English, this may be a formative challenge.

It is important for teachers to remember that by cherishing the varied resources ELLs bring to the classroom, and by being responsive to the unique needs of these students, the resulting instructional environment will be one that enhances the lives of all learners. Therefore, the importance of attaining this goal cannot be overemphasized, for without such associations, the classroom would most likely be described as "disconnected."

A "disconnected" classroom is one in which only *some* students feel connected. Annette Zehler (1994) states:

> For example, in the area of reading, research points out that it [reading] is a constructive process that involves building meaning not only from the words on the page, but also from one's related background knowledge. Often school texts assume a common experience that, in fact, is not shared by all students. If ELL students do not fully understand these texts, they are less likely to remember content material. (p. 3)

INTERCULTURAL UNDERSTANDING

In such a scenario, some ELLs may become inactive and therefore isolate themselves from opportunities to actively pursue the skills they need in order to learn. Other students may not believe their opinions are valued, so they may stop asking for help and/or answering questions. Still other students may be shy and believe they are in jeopardy of being ridiculed or put down for making a mistake. Without proper help, these students may just stop taking risks.

Teachers can assist ELLs by providing adequate wait time when requesting answers to questions. This allows students additional time to collect their thoughts and structure their answers. Recognizing that a student needs more time to respond sends a message to the student that you are interested in listening to what they have to say. Each student, at his or her own level of proficiency, should be given opportunities to communicate ideas, formulate questions, and use language for higher-order thinking (Zeller, 1994).

Vernon et al. (2000) suggest that teachers and students work together to build a classroom learning community where all students feel connected. In doing so, it is important that strategies be in place so that members of the class may

- be encouraged to participate and perform at their best;
- feel valued and appreciated for what they can contribute to the community;
- feel a sense of responsibility for the growth and learning of others in the class; and,
- feel safe and protected.

Positive behavior support

Horner, Sugai, Todd, and Lewis-Palmer (2005) state that as the expectations for schools have changed, the need has developed for a more encompassing, proactive approach for dealing with the wide range of challenges currently facing today's schools. It has become apparent that "knee-jerk" reactive consequences alone will not result in safe and orderly schools where a sense of community thrives. To attain this community, an alternative approach is required.

Positive Behavior Support (PBS) is such an approach because it creates a bridge where students experience success as they are connected to both the lessons being presented (education) and their classroom environment. Indeed, through PBS, students receive explicit information regarding both classroom and teacher expectations followed by consistent reinforcement/feedback via clearly structured class activities. When ELLs do not have to spend time "interpreting" expectations, procedures, and routines, they can focus their energies on the act of learning itself. Zehler (1994) provides several suggestions for the creation of an active learning environment for ELLs. These proposals which align with the basic tenets of PBS include:
- providing a clear acceptance of each student;
- making classroom activities structured and predictable; and,
- assisting students in knowing what is expected of them.

PBS alignment with ELL support

PBS has a substantial research base demonstrating its effectiveness among students with diverse disabilities and problem behaviors (Bambara, 2005). Horner et al. (2005) claim that PBS is not only for students with disabilities, but can be used with all students in schools today as they "come with a wide range of skills and from an increasing array of cultural, financial, and social contexts" (p. 360). The PBS continuum creates levels of support to decrease problem behavior, teach and reinforce pro-social skills, and improve the learning environment.

The conceptualization of PBS may be viewed as a three-tiered model that uses sequential prevention-focused strategies to reduce new and existing cases of problem behavior. PBS may also reduce the intensity and severity of such behaviors. The first tier of PBS targets the behavior of *all* children, involves *all* adults, applies to *all* settings and covers *all* times (Horner et al., 2005). This tier requires teachers to model and reinforce appropriate behavior in a predictable social environment. Since first tier instructors are quick to respond to problem behavior, every student has multiple opportunities to differentiate between what is defined as acceptable and what is defined as unacceptable behavior. Operating within tier one of PBS, students will gain recognition for exhibiting appropriate behavior. On this level, then, ELLs may be given explicit information regarding classroom/community expectations and then are provided multiple opportunities in which to practice them. Teachers can guide ELLs in appropriate behavior through genuine reinforcement and feedback.

The second tier of PBS comes into play when dealing with "children who are at risk for problem behavior, but for whom intensive, individualized intervention is not necessary" (Horner et.al., 2005, p. 362). In this tier, training focuses on targeted interventions so teams can work with students who display difficulties despite proactive school-wide prevention efforts. These students (10-15% of a school population) often exhibit both academic and behavioral challenges. ELLs at this stage may need further explanation of their roles and responsibilities. This may dictate the need for further social skills training, mentoring, behavior intervention programs, and academic support (May Institute, n.d.).

The third tier of PBS deals with students who have the most intense of behavior support needs. Within this level, concentrated individualized interventions are created for students exhibiting high-risk behavior. This tier requires intensive interventions that may include behavior support plans, social skills training, increased academic support, and/or mentoring. Teams are also created to work with students who exhibit difficulties despite more targeted interventions. These students comprise approximately 5% of a school population (May Institute, n.d.).

Learning community expectations

Teacher expectations regarding appropriate student behavior are often communicated to students in the form of classroom rules (Stronge, 2002). Clarifying what students are expected to do and helping them learn to do it is more effective than management that focuses on misbehavior after it occurs (Brophy, 2006). A good set of classroom rules is a critical component of PBS if it meets the criteria for effective rule design according to the literature. Specifically, each rule should begin with an action word, be stated positively, be observable and measurable, be specific in nature, yet general enough to be transferable across school settings

(Rademacher, Callahan, & Pederson, 1998). Classroom rules should also be reasonable and acceptable to diverse learners while defining what students are expected to do in order to be successful members of the learning community.

Rademacher, Pemberton, and Tyler-Wood (2006b) recommend that teachers use the term "expectations" to define student behavior for their students rather than "rules" for three reasons. First, students may view rules as negative and punitive in nature, rather than as guidelines for teaching them how to learn and get along with others. Second, expectations are more closely associated with the notion of what one can do in order to be personally responsible for one's own behavior. Third, some schools have a set of prescribed rules that each classroom teacher is expected to enforce, making it confusing to have two sets of rules. Thus, having a list of learning community expectations is more personal in nature and can be associated with, or compared to, the school rules if necessary.

To gain students' perceptions of a set of well-designed expectations, Rademacher et al. (2006b) administered a survey to 1,246 students that were representative of academic, ethnic, and gender diversity. The following set of Learning Community Expectations was deemed important by diverse students in grades three through eight as a reminder to them on how to learn and get along with others. See Figure 2.

Figure 2. Our Learning Community Expectations

Our Learning Community Expectations
• Enter the classroom quietly and prepared. • Follow directions. • Begin work promptly + stay on task + work until done.

> - Listen while others speak.
> - Signal to speak.
> - Use respectful language.
> - Keep hands, feet, and objects to yourself.

Rademacher et al. (2006a) conducted research with teachers and students to determine effective instructional procedures for enlisting students in the establishment of a classroom learning community. Once students understood the learning community concept, the teachers enlisted student participation in naming and agreeing upon a set of behavioral expectations to live respectfully, responsibly, and safely within their learning community as depicted in Figure 2 above.

The following section describes how "Lessons from the Geese" was used by these teachers to engage students in this process.

Using Lessons from the Geese

The story "Lessons from the Geese" appears in many places and in many versions on the internet. To find different presentations of this story, one may enter "Lessons from the Geese" or "The Goose Story" in an internet search engine. However, the researchers chose the one that appears at the beginning of this article to conduct their study.

As a result of the study, the following instructional procedures for using the story with your students are recommended. See Figure 3.

INTERCULTURAL UNDERSTANDING

Figure 3. Instructional Procedures for Using *Lessons from Geese*

Using *Lessons from the Geese* to Create a Learning Community

How to Prepare:

1. Create an overhead transparency of the story *Lessons from the Geese.*
 Optional: Prepare a copy of the story for each student in the class.

2. Create an overhead transparency and/or a poster of Our Learning Community Expectations as depicted in Figure 1.
 Optional: Prepare a copy of Our Learning Community Expectations for each student.

Instructional Procedures:

1. Introduce the concept of "learning community"
 * Define learning (finding out something new)
 * Define community (neighborhood, classroom, school, town, etc.)
 * Define learning community (a classroom where students care about each other and help one another learn)

2. Present the story *Lessons from the Geese*
 * Share the story *Lessons from the Geese* on the overhead with students
 * Use Figure 1 to guide students to identify and list the different ways geese act in their community as compared to how they can function as a learning community.

3. Gather student ideas for how a good learning community should operate.
 * Define responsible work habits (considering it our job to complete our work in a way that will help us learn).
 * Brainstorm ideas from students on how they must act in order to work responsibly and list them on the board.

INTERCULTURAL UNDERSTANDING

> * Define respect (thinking about we or someone else feels before we act).
> * Define physical safety (acting in a way so that no one in the learning community gets hurt).
> * Brainstorm ideas from students on how to show respect for other and list them on the board.
> * Brainstorm ideas from students on how they must act in order to be safe and list them on the board.
>
> 4. Present the overhead transparency and/or poster of Our Learning Community Expectations.
> * Tell students you believe this is a list of expectations that will help you teach and help them learn.
> * Compare your list with the lists generated by the students so the students can see how they are similar.
> * Enlist a commitment from the students to live by the expectations.
> * Give your commitment to help the students live by the expectations.
> * Hang Our Learning Community Expectations poster on the wall as a helpful reminder of how to work responsibly, respect one another, and be safe members of the learning community.

One reason Ms. Rader in the opening scenario was so successful at engaging her ELLs in classroom activities was that she created a learning environment which supported and sustained the principles inherent in both PBS and in *Lessons from the Geese*. For Jose, Maria, and Fernando, an explanation and demonstration of classroom rules and expected behaviors was critical. Ms. Rader also understood that specific information on routine tasks such as how to get the teacher's attention, how to pass out/in papers, how to transition between class activities, etc. enhanced the capability of Jose, Maria, and Fernando to function effectively within their classroom community.

Classroom teachers may add additional effectiveness and accessibility of their environment by displaying the expectations not only in English, but also in the ELLs' native language. Multilingual signs can make families as well as students feel more welcome in the school (Zehler, 1994). In addition, teachers may include the following instructional enhancements for ELLs that other students may find acceptable:

- a copy of *Lessons from the Geese* in the students' native language;
- a pictorial version of the story from the internet;
- an audio tape of the *Lessons from the Geese* in the students' native language;
- an illustration that compares the function of geese and students in a community;
- graphic organizers to clarify the concept of community, respect, and responsible work habits and safety;
- a note-taking outline for writing key words in each expectation;
- role-playing activities to practice each of the expectations;
- peer partners to brainstorm ideas for how to work and act responsibly; and
- student drawings of the classroom expectations.

Summary and conclusion

In summary, the need to create learning communities has never been greater because students come from a variety of cultures, racial/ethnic backgrounds, and religions. In spite of such diverse characteristics, students need to feel academically and socially "connected" to both education and the school in order to

INTERCULTURAL UNDERSTANDING

experience success. A "connected" learning community is an inclusive one in which teachers help students understand their roles and responsibilities, show students how to work in a self-directed manner, and enlist student participation in setting classroom expectations for working and getting along with others in a responsible, respectful, and safe manner.

PBS is a comprehensive behavior approach that is compatible with the notion of building an inclusive learning community for diverse learners. PBS is a three-tiered model that uses sequential prevention-focused strategies to reduce new and existing cases of problem behaviors. The second and third tiers of PBS require intensive specialized interventions for some students who are unable to adjust to the learning social demands of the classroom. However, the first tier is a proactive approach to classroom management because it requires teachers to model and reinforce appropriate behavior in a predictable social environment that is so important for ELLs.

Teacher expectations regarding appropriate behavior are often communicated to students in the form of classroom rules. Classroom rules should be reasonable and acceptable to diverse learners and define what students are expected to do in order to be successful members of the learning community. However, it is recommended that teachers use the term "expectations" to define student behavior for their students rather than "rules" because the term "expectations" is less punitive in nature, and is more closely associated with what one must personally do to be responsible. The learning community expectations can also be used in association with, or compared to, a set of prescribed school rules if necessary.

The story *Lessons from the Geese* can be used as an analogy to create an inclusive learning community. Comparing the functions of geese in their community with how students live together in their learning community offers a concrete way to engage students in the process. Once students understand the concept of the learning community, it is recommended that they participate in naming and agreeing on the set of learning community expectations as presented in this article. Comparing Functions of Geese and Students in a Community (Figure 1) offers ideas on how to use the *Lessons from the Geese* story. Our Learning Community Expectations (Figure 2) presents the set of classroom expectations that can be shared with students after they understand the concept of the learning community. Using *Lessons from the Geese* to Create a Learning Community (Figure 3) offers preparation and instructional procedures for using the story and the set of expectations to create an inclusive learning community.

In conclusion, this article offered sound procedures for creating an inclusive learning community that includes a set of learning expectations based on responsible work habits, respect, and safety. Inappropriate behavior often occurs because students do not *know* a more appropriate way to achieve a particular outcome. Rather than relying on power and enforcement of punitive models of control, teachers can create an environment where all members feel safe and protected so that inappropriate behaviors are less likely to occur in the first place. However, merely agreeing upon, and posting expectations for the learning community may not be enough for some students. It is further recommended that teachers model for students how to follow the expectations, as well as engage them in learning activities that will promote mastery of them.

It is also important to note that while establishing clear guidelines for behavior is important, it is only one aspect of a well-managed classroom. Teachers must also consider other factors in their overall management of the learning community. For example, a PBS approach will require teachers to examine other environmental variables such as the physical setting, task demands, curriculum, instruction, and individualized reinforcement. A supportive learning environment is possible when teachers are adept planners in each of these areas as well.

Finally, while the contents of this article primarily focused on using ideas and procedures derived from the *Lessons from the Geese* story to students in K-12 settings, the framework is equally applicable to adult learners. For example, in undergraduate education classes at the university level, preservice teachers often matriculate through their prescribed courses as members of cohorts. When cohorts function as true classroom communities, opportunities exist where skills such as the following can be developed and nurtured:

- sharing a common vision;
- sharing a common direction;
- sharing leadership tasks;
- understanding and practicing interdependency;
- giving aid to others;
- accepting help from others;
- learning the power of encouragement;
- taking turns handling more difficult matters; and
- staying together while navigating both effortless and demanding experiences.

Would not beginning teachers enter the classroom better prepared to utilize the diverse gifts, talents, and resources embodied by their students if they had experienced and practiced first-hand, as student themselves, the principles embodied in *Lessons from the Geese*? Truly, the seeds of today become the flowers of tomorrow.

References

Bambara, L. (2005). Evolution of positive behavior support. In L. Bambara & L. Kern (Eds.), *Supports for students with problem behaviors: Designing positive behavior plans* (pp. 1-20). New York: The Guilford Press.

Brophy, J. E. (2006). History of research on classroom management. In C. M. Evertson & C. S. Weinstein (Eds.), *Handbook of classroom management: Research, practice, and contemporary issues* (1st ed., pp. 17-46). Mahwah, NJ: Lawrence Erlbaum Associates.

Horner, R., Sugai, G., Todd, A., & Lewis-Palmer, T. (2005). Schoolwide positive behavior support. In L. Bambara & L. Kern (Eds.), *Individualized supports for students with problem behaviors: Designing positive behavior plans* (pp. 359-390). New York: The Guilford Press.

May Institute (n.d.). In Pollack E. G. (Ed.), *Positive behavior support services: Improving learning and behavior*. Randolph, MA: Author. Retrieved February 7, 2007, from http://www.mayinstitute.org/pdfs/PBSOverview306Final.pdf

McNeish, R. (2006). Lessons from the geese. In J. A. Rademacher, J. B. Pemberton, & G. Cheever (Eds.), *Focusing together: Promoting self-management skills in the classroom* (pp. 54). Lawrence, KS: Edge Enterprises.

Rademacher, J. A., Callahan, K., & Pederson-Seeley, V. (1998). How do your classroom rules measure up? *Intervention in School and Clinic, 33*(5), 284-288.

Rademacher, J. A., Pemberton, J. B., & Cheever, G. (2006a). *Focusing together: Promoting self-management skills in the classroom*. Lawrence, KS: Edge Enterprises.

Rademacher, J. A., Pemberton, J. B., & Tyler-Wood, T. (2006b). *Giving students a voice: What diverse learners think about classroom rules*. Unpublished manuscript.

Stronge, J. H. (2002). *Qualities of effective teachers*. Alexandria, VA: Association for Supervision and Curriculum Development.

Turnbull, A. P., Turnbull, H. R., & Wehmeyer, M. L. (2007). *Exceptional lives: Special education in today's schools* (5th ed.). Upper Saddle River, NJ: Prentice-Hall.

Vernon, F., Schumaker, J., & Deshler, D. (2000). *Talking together*. Lawrence, KS: Edge Enterprises.

Zehler, Annette. (1994). Working with English language learners: Strategies for elementary and middle school teachers. NCBE Program Information Guide Series (19). Retrieved March 10, 2007 from http://www.ncela.gwu.edu/pubs/pigs/pig19.htm

The Community Plunge: A Cultural Immersion Experience For Preservice Teachers

Ron Wilhelm
University of North Texas
Melinda F. Cowart
Texas Woman's University
Joyce Rademacher
Texas Woman's University

Demographic changes in U. S. public school student populations, as a result of desegregation and the influx of Asian and Latin American immigrants since the last two decades of the twentieth century, have produced a major debate about appropriate U. S. pedagogical focus. Should schools in the U. S. continue some form of the early twentieth century "Americanization" pedagogy or should they engage in culturally relevant curriculum and instruction that privileges the cultural knowledge students possess? The increasing demographic disparity between a predominantly white, middle class, female teaching force and a culturally and linguistically diverse, poor and working class public school student population has prompted both university teacher preparation programs and public school districts to reconsider not only the knowledge and skills needed by new teachers but also the appropriate formats for imparting that knowledge in a manner that cultivates cultural sensitivity.

For some advocates of urban educational reform, culturally responsive teaching represents " . . . one kind of special effort that can reduce miscommunication by teachers and students, foster trust, and prevent the genesis of conflict that moves rapidly beyond intercultural misunderstanding to bitter struggles of negative identity exchange between some students and their teachers" (Erickson, 1992, p. 394). G. Pritchy Smith (1998) has identified four premises that constitute the basis of culturally responsive pedagogy: (a) culture influences the way students learn; (b) teachers must understand the culture of their students and translate this understanding into instructional practice; (c) much of the difficulty ethnic/racial minority and language minority students experience is due to cultural incongruity between the school's white middle class culture and the students' culture; and (d) classroom teachers can create the desired environment of cultural synchronization or congruence by culturally contextualizing the teaching-learning process. Educators employing a culturally responsive approach typically demonstrate several common instructional attitudes or behaviors including: (a) a belief in the social construction of knowledge by the students and teachers (Ladson-Billings, 1994), (b) the establishment of a collaborative learning environment (Ladson-Billings, 1994; Hollins, 1996), (c) the inclusion of the students' cultural knowledge and home culture, particularly the language, as an integral part of the official curriculum (Torres-Guzman, 1992; Jordan, Tharp & Baird-Vogt, 1992; Mitchell, 1992; Ladson-Billings, 1994; Delpit, 1995; Hollins, 1996), (d) a critically challenging approach to the social status quo (Grant, 1994; Ladson-Billings, 1994; Delpit, 1995), (e) an emphasis on high learning standards for all students (Ladson-Billings, 1994; Delpit, 1995), and (f) the use of constant, critical self-reflection to monitor their own cultural biases and development of cross-cultural literacy (Delpit, 1995; Hollins, 1996; Hoffman, 1996; Bradfield-Kreider, 1999).

INTERCULTURAL UNDERSTANDING

How to develop future teachers with culturally responsive characteristics represents the major challenge for teacher preparation programs and public school districts. Ladson-Billings (1994) has detailed eloquently the difficulties in molding culturally relevant teachers:

> Most teacher candidates do not need an immersion experience in white middle class culture because they are either products of it or have been acculturated and/or assimilated enough to negotiate it successfully. However, when beginning teachers come into minority communities, many are unable to understand the students' home language, social interaction patterns, histories, and cultures. Thus they cannot truly educate the students. Their perceptions of deficiency and competence are socially and culturally constructed. Without greater exposure to the students' culture teachers lack the tools with which to make sense of much that transpires in the classroom.
> Further, they cannot serve effectively in a decontextualized manner. Immersion in the community to learn who the community leaders are, where the community centers are, which people command respect, what matters to the children in the community, all provide teachers with needed information about how to work *with* rather than *against* the community. (p. 134)

In this chapter, the authors describe one strategy they have called "the community plunge," which is designed to promote culturally responsive teaching in preservice educators.

The plunge rationale

Cultural immersion experiences have long been used by government agencies and businesses to prepare their personnel for cross cultural work. The community plunge constitutes an adaptation of cultural immersion for preservice teachers from the University of North Texas in an inner city neighborhood in Dallas, Texas. This activity, a type of cultural scavenger hunt, is intended to provide novice educators (also called interns) with an introductory experience in the community served by the schools in which they will student teach. (Although Wilhelm originally developed the plunge activity for an inner city teaching experience, Boutte (1999) has expanded the Dallas design with guidelines for educators in any location.)

Through participation in the plunge and subsequent group debriefing, the interns gather initial information about the places in which their future students and families live, play, worship, shop, secure social services, or just *hang out* or *cruise*. The interns are encouraged to use and build on their new knowledge in their lesson plans and interactions with their students throughout their student teaching practicum. The authors concur with Delpit (1994):

> If we do not have some knowledge of children's lives outside of the realms of paper-and-pencil work, and even outside of their classrooms, then we cannot know their strengths. Not knowing students' strengths leads to our "teaching down" to children from communities that are culturally different from that of the teachers in the school. Because teachers do not want to tax what they believe to be these students' lower abilities, they end up teaching less when, in actuality, these students need *more* of what school has to offer. (p. 173)

Delpit further stressed the importance of including community learning experiences in novice teachers' preparation. She argued, "It is unreasonable to expect that teachers will automatically value the knowledge that parents and community members bring to the education of diverse children if valuing such knowledge has not been modelled [sic] for them by those from whom they learn to teach" (p. 179).

An additional plunge learning objective involves helping the interns reduce their apprehensions about the inner city neighborhood and their future students. Most of the interns live in middle class suburbs surrounding Dallas and rarely venture into the inner city. Many have developed media-generated, negative stereotypes of the Oak Cliff area in which they will student teach. By engaging in a community plunge during the first week of their student teaching practicum, the interns must confront their misinformation and stereotypes so that they might overcome their fear of the area residents, particularly their students.

The plunge is the first of several group experiential learning activities designed to help interns develop critical communities that provide these predominantly ". . . monocultural teachers a safe environment in which to confront and broaden their ethnocentric cultural and professional identities and to develop the collective social change strategies and support structures to operationalize reconstructed notions of their role in the 'teaching, and learning enterprise,' thereby counteracting the resistance to multicultural change" (Bradfield-Kreider, 1999, p. 31).

Designing and organizing the plunge

For the plunge, the interns are divided randomly into groups of four or five students per group. Each group receives a map of the area, bus schedule, and a distinct route description including a cultural questionnaire (See Appendix A) to be completed during the exploration of the group's particular route. The questionnaire format guides the interns to uncover specific examples of cultural universals including material culture, religion and world view, aesthetics, social conflict, language, social organization, education, recreation, and economic organization. The theoretical framework for the topics of exploration is derived from a description of the nine universals of culture by Cleveland, Craven and Danfelser (1979).

Before embarking on the plunge, each group reviews the route description, map and bus schedule and identifies each member's responsibilities, whether as a *Tour Guide*, *Travel Agent*, *Recorder*, or *Reporter* as described in a handout about the community plunge activity (See Appendix B). The faculty members provide the interns with school phone numbers and their cell phone numbers in case of an emergency. At least one person in each group carries a cell phone. One faculty member is always near a phone during the morning exploration and another faculty member travels in a vehicle to check periodically on the groups' progress and activities along each route.

Traveling together on foot and by public transportation, each group explores a different route in the area during a four-hour period in the morning. Because many of the interns have grown up in the suburbs, some experience challenges as they attempt to read bus schedules and negotiate public transportation. Faculty members urge the groups to undertake the plunge with sensitivity and creativity as they explore locations on their route and to converse about the area with people they meet at bus stops, in shops, along the streets, or in restaurants. The majority population of the area explored is Latino with Spanish as the dominant language. Monolingual English-speaking interns must discover ways to converse with the Spanish speakers they meet along their route. Those interns who are familiar with the area are invited to engage in the plunge with new, outsider's eyes and also to lead their group to interesting sites not listed on their route itinerary. As they meet people along the route, most interns have found once they explain they are student teachers out exploring and trying to learn more about the community in which they will teach, the shopkeepers and social service workers warmly receive them.

Following a morning of exploration, including a mandated lunch in any one of a number of local ethnic restaurants, the interns reassemble for an afternoon debriefing session (See Appendix C for a list of debriefing questions). Faculty members have found the debriefing period essential to help interns process and probe their attitudes, feelings, and new insights about the area and their future students. In particular, faculty members encourage interns to challenge their own and one another's perceptions, information, and misinformation about the area and their students. This debriefing session is designed to help the interns understand that the process of reflective thinking requires that they must "expose their thinking to others and open themselves to criticism from peers as well as from authority" (Ross & Hannay, 1986, p. 13). Bradfield-Kreider (1999) has detailed the significance of supportive communities of critique, "We benefit from continually reconstructing our cultural identities and our roles as educators and cultural workers, confronting biases and blind spots, and filling in the gaps in our knowledge base" (p. 31).

Debriefing the plunge

The information presented in this section has been compiled from debriefing sessions, conducted as structured group interviews each semester since the fall of 1994, and includes both a summary of general reflections of more than 100 interns as well as some of their specific comments. The debriefing session consists of a

INTERCULTURAL UNDERSTANDING

jigsaw group strategy in which members of each group first meet together to reflect on what they learned about their particular route. Then, all interns are regrouped randomly into three or four groups, each facilitated by a faculty member or selected intern. Using the interview protocol in Appendix C, each facilitator directs the interns' analysis of their morning exploration experience. Each group keeps a written record of the interns' thoughts and findings. The information presented in this section is derived from those written records and from audiotapes of the sessions.

<u>Problems encountered along the routes</u>

The principal problems reported by the interns related to the bus schedules and routes. Comments such as "We got on the wrong bus" or "We missed the bus" or "The bus route had changed" were common. The facilitators directing the debriefing session helped the interns consider what it would be like to arrange one's life around dependence on public transportation. In particular, faculty members prompted interns to reflect on how dependence on public transportation might impact their students and parents. After waiting for a late bus, one intern seeking certification in grades 8-12 laughingly commented that if one of his students told him that he was late because of the bus, he [the intern] would accept that as a possible excuse for tardiness. Another intern, who waited long periods for buses that never appeared, reflected on his experience:

> It made me think about people who have to depend on it to get to work all the time and how, whether it's the child's parents or when they're coming home to meet them at home or whatever. There's some questions there. They may or may not be there on time because of that bus. We went to get our first bus and we were there on time and it never showed up. We just waited another 30 or 20 minutes, but it just never

INTERCULTURAL UNDERSTANDING

showed up and then at other times the bus was exactly to the minute on time. One problem encountered by some groups involved the shops on their itinerary.

Occasionally shops were closed on the day of the plunge even though it was the middle of the typical business week. As interns compared the businesses on their various routes, they came to understand that the area contains a large number of family-owned stores and shops such as bridal salons, piñata shops, tire and auto repair shops, antique stores, and restaurants. Invariably, the family-owned, small business culture of Oak Cliff makes a profound impression on suburban interns accustomed to strip malls and chain restaurants. One intern reported a sign at one closed business:

> Apparently there was a barber who worked inside there [a neighborhood business] who had just died. They had a note up there to all the people who cared for him, who loved him, and all who had come by to visit him when he was sick, that they appreciated the support and everything else, "Thank you," and like that. You don't see that where I live. I noticed that the [Oak Cliff] community seemed to be a little more tight, by seeing things like that, than mine is. A second business-related problem centered around the fact that often the store or shop staff spoke only Spanish. Many interns quickly learned they were disadvantaged by their English monolingual status when they attempted to read signs or to question store employees about certain services or products. At times interns interpreted store employees' responses to their presence and queries as unfriendly or even rude. A discussion of these experiences led the interns to develop empathy for the challenges facing their Spanish monolingual students.

INTERCULTURAL UNDERSTANDING

<u>Learning related to city services, code enforcement, and social conflict</u>

On each route, the groups are directed to identify evidence of wheel chair accessibility to sidewalks, businesses and restaurants and also evidence of lack of code enforcement. Typically, the interns notice a distinct difference between the deteriorated condition of the streets and sidewalks in the working class neighborhood immediately surrounding the elementary and middle schools in which they will student teach and the maintained state of the more middle class neighborhoods along other parts of their routes. At this point in the discussion, the faculty members help the interns understand that many of the residents in the working class neighborhood are undocumented immigrants who are wary of pressing government authorities for improvement of city services or code enforcement. One intern's remarks are typical of the observations made: "I thought it was interesting how the houses would change within just a couple of blocks. The houses would go from very nice to drastically lower economic and back up again." A related exchange between two interns illustrates a similar observation and points to the intern's initial efforts to critically analyze her experiences:

> We noticed that within two blocks you could totally change neighborhoods. One would be a safer looking and a more prosperous neighborhood and they had sidewalks that were intact. But then you walked down a couple of blocks to lower income houses and their sidewalks were all broken up. And I, the only thing we could think, was that they didn't know the processes to go through in order to complain to the city.

A second intern responded:

INTERCULTURAL UNDERSTANDING

That's a polite way to put it. No, I mean, I'm just saying that just shows you that there's clout in certain neighborhoods that can get things done and that's politics.

Notably, this exchange serves also as an example of the importance of this initial debriefing activity to create an atmosphere of critical reflection in which the interns may challenge each other's perceptions and misperceptions about the community or their students.

As they reflect on evidence of social conflict, most often the interns report sighting gang-related graffiti on wooden fences, abandoned houses, and businesses as well as seeing a preponderance of metal security bars on the windows of many homes and businesses. Clearly gang activity is present in the area and in all three schools in which the interns teach. One plunge route takes a group of interns to a police storefront facility to learn about the various anti-gang programs and other services offered to the children and adult residents of the area.

Learning related to the types of social services in the area

Each route contains at least one agency or organization that offers some type of social services to residents of Oak Cliff. By talking with the staff of area social service organizations, the interns learn how agencies respond to the pressing human needs of the area's residents. During the debriefing session interns share their new information about agencies such as the Salvation Army [clothing assistance, meals for the elderly, inexpensive after school day care and tutoring], Catholic Charities [food bank, immigration counseling, clothing assistance], Dallas Intertribal Center [employment counseling, medical and dental assistance, housing and clothing assistance], WIC (Women, Infants, and Children

INTERCULTURAL UNDERSTANDING

Program)], Weiss Recreation Center [recreational activities for children and elderly adults, citizenship classes, English classes, community organization meetings], Dallas Legal Hospice [legal aid to terminal AIDS patients], African American Health Coalition [counseling, housing assistance, AIDS awareness outreach and counseling], and the Oak Cliff Community Services Center [free income tax counseling, assistance to the homeless, food pantry, housing assistance, after school tutoring and children's camps]. They also gain important practical knowledge about agencies to which they might refer their students and families. One intern expressed his revelation of the complexities of Oak Cliff:

> One thing that changed the most for me, I think, was I originally, if anyone had asked me before I came down here to see any of the schools or anything, "What's Oak Cliff like?" I would've probably thought, "Well it's got a whole lot of bad people down there." And now I think it's got a whole lot of good people with just a few bad people who make the news because it's what you hear. Every time you hear a community being lambasted by some news media person about "Oh, they have so much crime down there," you always see the mothers get on there and say, "You don't know our community. You're not down there. We do all kinds of great things. It's just a few people who are doing something wrong who make the news." And now I see where they're coming from. I mean, there's a lot of people trying to help people out there, but there's also graffiti here, graffiti there, broken windows here, broken windows there. We saw one building, someone had painted on the side of the building, "Please stop the shooting, we all need the peace."

INTERCULTURAL UNDERSTANDING

<u>Learning related to cultural differences between interns' communities and Oak Cliff</u>

One of the debriefing questions asks the interns to compare and contrast their home community with what they have experienced on the plunge. The question is intended to help them explore the concept of positionality or an individual's socioeconomic and political privileges and limitations due to gender, ethnicity, and social class. Faculty members guide interns to think critically about both their own positionality and that of their students. As they discuss what exists in their home communities, but not in Oak Cliff, and what is found in Oak Cliff, but not in their communities, the interns uncover important cultural patterns. Several of the comments below illustrate how the interns expressed their understanding of elements of positionality.

> Even in the homes, even in the places where it's obvious these people don't have very much money, the yards are as neat as they can be, the houses, of course you can't see inside, but outside things are kept up. I have just been very impressed. There seems to be a real difference in this area and the area that I'm from in the poverty-stricken areas. Here there seems to be more of a pride. I don't know what it is but it's very definitely different.

> Our neighborhood tends to be almost solely residential. You have to have a car to be able to get to the store, there's no public transit. Everything is really far to walk to so a car is demanded in that area. And here I'm not sure, it seems like things were within walking distance to get to a store, albeit maybe a convenience store, a 7-11 or something, but you could get to different places within walking distance. There's more businesses and I'm not sure that that's a bad thing.

INTERCULTURAL UNDERSTANDING

There's more home-cooked restaurants. Where I live, you've got your chain restaurants and your restaurant row and there's no cafes, no mom and pop stores at all.

I saw a lot of front yards that were fenced in, and that it's chain link and you can see they're not trying to keep the world out. Where we are, everybody has their privacy fences in the back trying to keep everybody out because, heaven forbid, that we communicate. But it didn't seem to be that. There were a lot of chain link fences in the front yards and that was in the older homes. Sometimes I felt as if I was in another country when we were going down because everything was in Spanish a lot of times.

I've never seen pigs' heads or cows' heads [in the grocery store meat sections] before. I was telling my group that this is my first view of Oak Cliff. Usually I just zoom by, you know. I just go where I have to go. I see it differently now because I mean it's like homey, I guess, you know. You go into the stores and you find what you need and the people, well the people treated us really nice. I mean I'd come back again if I needed to get like a piñata or christening gowns and stuff like that that I can't find anywhere else.

It was also surprising to see that religion is just a really big part of this community. I mean, the different churches, the different stores. We went into Fiesta [a large supermarket] and they had, you know, statues of the Virgin Mary, not the Virgin Mary, but different virgins and the saints on the shelves. And that's everywhere.

The previous remarks illustrate initial steps in the interns' journey to understand their students' world in relation to their own. Delpit (1994) has commented on the effort needed for cross-cultural understanding:

> Learning to interpret across cultures demands reflecting on our own experiences, analyzing our own culture, examining

and comparing varying perspectives. We must consciously and voluntarily make our cultural lenses apparent. Engaging in the hard work of seeing the world as others see it must be a fundamental goal for any move to reform the education of teachers and their assessment. (p. 151)

Building on the community plunge learning

One of the primary learning goals of the community plunge included providing the interns with the opportunity to understand the practical classroom usefulness of knowledge about their students' cultural backgrounds. Three debriefing questions prompted reflection in three related areas: (a) how might the interns build on their plunge experience to further their own understanding of their students' cultural backgrounds, (b) how might the interns situate their newly acquired cultural information in their teaching and curriculum in order to elicit and build on their students' cultural capital and enhance their learning, and (c) how might the interns use the resources and information gained during the plunge to validate their students' world and help them question the social status quo.

Interns generated several sound ideas about how they could learn more about their students' lives and cultures:

> I would have liked to have more time to really talk to the people. It was a nice tour and now I'd like to spend some more time just talking with residents. It was a wonderful taste of Oak Cliff, but, I mean, you can't learn everything in a morning. I just think that I'm going to go back some more and look around and talk to people.
>
> This may sound stupid, but I'd like to come out here at night and see what the difference is between the night and the day. I mean, any place is dangerous to go walking around,

you know, at night, but I think that there's maybe a different atmosphere during the night than there is during the day.

I'd like to ask the kids their point of view on what they experience when they go to the different places. Sometimes they see things in a completely different way or they may have more insight into it.

One possibility for getting a better feel of the area is to actually take a tour of it with somebody who lives here. We were all outsiders and we were just wandering around on a prescribed route, but actually going out with somebody who knows the area with someone who could say "Oh, that's we're thus and so happened or this or that and the other," who could give us like a more guided tour. You could see it through their eyes.

One European American intern, who upon her graduation at midyear became a teacher of African American history at a south Dallas high school, so valued her community plunge experience that she planned to have her future students design and lead her on a plunge of their neighborhood.

A second debriefing question helped the interns focus on how they might incorporate the information gained through the plunge in order to build on their students' cultural knowledge. Some of their comments below evince a seminal, yet naïve and somewhat superficial awareness of how best to use their recently acquired knowledge to help their students connect with curricular content. Nevertheless, they appear to have captured the importance of restructuring their curriculum ". . . so as to build on students' past experiences" (Delpit, 1994, p. 125).

> Well, you wouldn't wanna, like I'm from the country, you wouldn't wanna bring a bunch of stuff they wouldn't know about, you know, animals, you know, and that sort of things.

INTERCULTURAL UNDERSTANDING

You'd wanna bring to your classroom stuff that makes them feel comfortable, you know, about their culture and the things that are around them.

You can use things from their community that they understand and base your lessons on that. You don't need to educate them about some other community, you know.

I was gonna say you could compare things. You could, you know, talk about their supermarket then you could, you know, talk about different ones that are in the U. S. or different cultures, for that matter. You know, how they, like, set up. Like, the French, for example, you know, have separate bakeries, separate fish, separate meat. I mean everything is very different. Then you've got the *supermercado* that's got more produce and vegetables than anything.

You'd wanna refer to places that are in here. Like, you don't wanna talk about, like, if you were doing an economics lesson to use the Gap, a chain clothing store found in malls outside of Oak Cliff, as an experience. You'd wanna use, you know, one of the bridal shops or the Rexall, a chain drug store, one of the businesses located here they can relate to.

I thought about class projects that students could do to support the Salvation Army like the elderly, like, you know, make them cards at special, you know, holidays.

I just think that the important thing is to realize that they have their own world here and that they've got components for everything they do in life just like in different parts of Dallas and the world and just to use their universe in your classroom.

The interns' reflections indicate an initial, basic understanding of culturally relevant teaching described by Hollins (1996):

> Curriculum content in general should be meaningful and relevant for all youngsters. The curriculum should be

explicitly related to the daily lives of the students and they should understand how it relates to their future adult lives. The curriculum should help youngsters maintain a sense of identity and personal worth and a feeling of connectedness to people like themselves as well as those who are different. Youngsters should find a positive representation of their cultural heritage within the curriculum. (p. 155)

The challenge for faculty members is to build on these initial reactions in order to help interns deepen their critical abilities and understanding as they learn how to select and organize curricular content throughout the semester.

Another major goal of the community plunge experience, to reduce the interns' apprehension and increasing their comfort with their students, when achieved, lays the foundation for a rich student teaching experience. The interns' reflections in the following section point to the plunge as one strategy to foster a critical, questioning attitude (Ladson-Billings, 1994) in the interns.

Changes in perceptions of Oak Cliff

Bradfield-Kreider (1999) has noted the importance of faculty mediation of cultural immersion experiences: "Mediated cultural immersions offer opportunities for teachers to gain a critical regard for social justice and a multicultural vision for educational equity and to develop the accompanying political strategies to begin their cultural work" (p. 32). In the comments below, the interns express their newly acquired understanding of the environment in which they will student teach. The underlying themes of racism and classism in some of the comments are taken up in subsequent sessions in which the UNT faculty members guide the interns to examine the construction of their own prejudices and benefits from

INTERCULTURAL UNDERSTANDING

white privilege as well as to analyze the specific ways that institutionalized prejudice affects student success.

Whenever you hear "Oak Cliff," you tend to think of the crime and the bad areas. Whenever you see this different area and this different culture and you get out in it, you realize it's, you know, I guess, like the same culture you live in.

The media makes it sound like you wouldn't even want to walk on the street; you don't want to do anything. I mean, I was real apprehensive when I heard that we were just going to walk down the streets in these neighborhoods. I mean because, the media, all we ever hear about the media is someone got killed here, someone had something else happen. You never hear anything good so you automatically assume if you've never been here that that is the way it is.

I was going to say that I thought that Oak Cliff was all African American because I was surprised at the large Hispanic community. Another thing that surprises me just driving around coming here to school is that Amelia Earhart [an elementary school in west Dallas just north of the Oak Cliff area] is probably 90 or 95% African American students where we are all Latino so they obviously have segregation here as far as, I mean, blacks live in a certain area, African Amer... or the Hispanics in another area, and then you've got all the older homes where a lot of old [white] people live.

Well, if you talk to some people and you tell them about Oak Cliff, they get the idea like of total gang wars, big city, horrible, urban, you know, the worst you can imagine. It's really not. I mean there probably is that stuff sometimes in some areas but that exists almost in any city anywhere. I mean it's not the horrible place that a lot of people think it is.

I felt safe like she did because I didn't wanna take my purse with me. I just left my purse here and left my books or whatever. I just took a little pouch with me. But I'm like what would have been the big deal if I had taken my purse anyway.

These interns' remarks underscore the power of the plunge activity to cause novice educators to question the dominant, media-reinforced view of a particular segment of the population. Delpit (1995) wrote about the hope embedded in alternative university education experiences such as the plunge:

> Finally, organizing the university classroom so that all students' stories are heard and all opinions valued may make inroads into that persistent scourge of American society, racial prejudice and discrimination—'modern' or otherwise. As white students and faculty learn to listen to and respect the words of people of color, perhaps they will carry these new attitudes of openness and acceptance of difference to other aspects of their lives, and certainly to their future teaching. (p. 127)

Implications of the community plunge experience for teacher education programs

Over the past four decades, a considerable amount of literature has developed related to cross-cultural training for businesses, the Peace Corps and diplomatic corps. Cultural immersion experiences and simulation activities receive prominent coverage in this literature. Less information is available related to cross-cultural, experiential learning activities for teachers in training. For example, the relationship between a reduction in interns' fear of the teaching environment and of their prospective students and the novice teachers' future success in student teaching appears to be important, albeit unmeasured except by anecdotal evidence. The value of a community plunge experience emerges as evident in many of the interns' new revelations contained in this chapter. Indeed, several veteran teachers who serve as mentors of the interns have expressed a desire to participate in a community plunge in the area even though some of them have taught in the school for more than twenty years.

A cultural immersion experience, even in cases in which the student teachers hail from cultural and class backgrounds similar to those of their students, offers the opportunity to view one's community anew with outsiders' eyes. The insights gained through such experiential learning provide student teachers the possibility of connecting the important relationship between schooling and the community culture in which it occurs. As they began to teach, some interns drew upon their plunge learning in impromptu ways during class discussions with their own students. For example, one African American intern, seeking secondary certification in sociology, led his senior students in a discussion about social rituals. He later described to other interns and his instructor how the girls excitedly engaged in a conversation about the upcoming senior prom, which the intern had likened to a *quinceañera* (fifteenth birthday celebration, a kind of coming of age party for many Latinas). One surprised young Latina asked him how he knew about *quinceañeras*. The intern responded by describing his plunge experience earlier that semester and told of his visit during to a local bridal shop that also sold *quinceañera* dresses. His comments opened up a cultural space for the girl, who, according to the intern, rarely spoke in class. She began to share memories of her own *quinceañera* celebration a few years earlier. The intern reported the girl later told him his class was the best class she had in all her high school years. This intern's unplanned remark during a class discussion that day reveals the power of connecting with and privileging the cultural knowledge and backgrounds of students as part of the official classroom discourse and curricular content.

Although that intern serendipitously happened upon a teachable moment, the instructors involved in the plunge also required interns to create a unit of study titled "Oak Cliff, the hidden city." The goal of the unit was for the interns to learn to plan for the systematic inclusion of the community and students' home cultures in math, reading, social studies, and science lessons. The process by which interns learn to build upon and to incorporate plunge experiences and information in their daily curriculum and instruction merits further attention and detailed study.

We call on the novice teachers to undertake the community plunge with sensitivity and creativity. As teacher educators we should do no less in designing learning activities to help our students bridge what, at first glance, appears to be insuperable cultural chasms. For if we fail to accomplish that goal, we risk the possibility of producing perhaps caring, but culturally inept teachers, ill prepared to face the complex and challenging needs of today's learners.

References

Boutte, G., (Ed.). (1999). *Multicultural education: Raising consciousness.* Belmont, CA: Wadsworth Publishing Co.

Bradfield-Kreider, P. (1999). Mediated cultural immersion and antiracism: An opportunity for monocultural preservice teachers to begin the dialogue. *Multicultural Perspectives 1* (2), 29-32.

Cleaveland, A., Craven, J. & Danfelser, M. (1979). Universals of culture. *Intercom*, 92-93, 1-72.

Delpit, L. (1995). *Other people's children: Cultural conflict in the classroom.* New York: The New Press.

Erickson, F. (1992). Transformation and school success: The politics and culture of educational achievement. In J. Kretovics & E. J. Nussel (Eds.), *Transforming urban education* (pp. 375-395). Needham Heights, MA: Allyn and Bacon.

Grant, C. A. (1994). Urban teachers: Their new colleagues and curriculum. In J. K. & E. J. Nussel (Eds.), *Transforming urban education* (pp. 315-326). Needham Heights, MA: Allyn and Bacon.

Hoffman, D. (1996). Culture and self in multicultural education: Reflections on discourse, text, and practice. *American Educational Research Journal 33* (3), 545-569.

Hollins, E. R. (1996). *Culture in school learning: Revealing the deep meaning.* Mahwah, NJ: Lawrence Erlbaum Associates, Publishers.

Jordan, C., Tharp, R. G., & Baird-Vogt, L. (1992). 'Just open the door:' Cultural compatibility and classroom rapport. In M. Saravia-Shore & S. F. Arvizu (Eds.), *Cross-cultural literacy: Ethnographies of communication in multiethnic classrooms*, (pp. 3-18). New York: Garland Publishing, Inc.

Ladson-Billings, G. (1994). *The dreamkeepers: Successful teachers of African American children.* San Francisco: Jossey-Bass Inc., Publishers.

Minutaglio, B. & Williams, H. (1990). *The hidden city: Oak Cliff, Texas.* Dallas, TX: Elmwood Press and the Oak Cliff Conservation League.

Mitchell, V. (1992). African-American students in exemplary urban high schools. In M. Saravia-Shore and S.F. Arvizu (Eds), *Cross-cultural literacy: Ethnographies of communication in multiethnic classrooms*, (pp. 19-36). New York: Garland Publishing, Inc.

Oak Cliff Chamber of Commerce. (n. d.). *Greater Oak Cliff Economic and CommunityProfile.* (Brochure). Dallas, TX: Author.

Ross, E. W., & Hannay, L. M. (1986). Towards a critical theory of reflective inquiry. *Journal of Teacher Education, 37*, 9-15.

Smith, G. P. (1998). *Common sense about uncommon knowledge: The knowledge bases for diversity.* Washington, DC: American Association of Colleges of Teacher Education.

Torres-Guzman, M. E. (1992). Stories of hope in the midst of despair: Culturally responsive education for Latino students in an alternative high school in New York City. In M. Saravia-Shore & S. F. Arvizu (Eds.), *Cross-cultural literacy: Ethnographies of communication in multiethnic classrooms* (pp. 477-490). New York: Garland Publishing, Inc.

Appendix A

Route #2 Questionnaire

From Cowart Elementary, proceed east on Bentley five blocks to Superior. As you walk attend to the following aspects of the neighborhood:

    How would you describe the dominant architecture?
    Are most of the houses wood frame or brick?
    What types of adornments or decorations are visible in the yards or houses?
    What patriotic or religious symbols did you see in the yards or houses?
    What is your assessment of the physical condition of most of the homes?
    Approximately how many homes were vacant? For Rent? For Sale?
    Were the sidewalks wheel-chair accessible at the corners?
    Based on the houses you observed, how would you classify the average standard of living in the neighborhood?
    What evidence of social problems did you see?

INTERCULTURAL UNDERSTANDING

When you reach Superior, cross to the east side of the street and take the DART bus No. 510 "Sunset" (destination 8th & Corinth Station). Be certain to notice the houses and businesses along the route. Converse with other riders about where they are going or how often they ride the bus. Get off at Jefferson Blvd. and Lancaster. Explore the following businesses in the area:

1. Pan African Connection Bookstore (612 E. Jefferson): What books/authors do you find who deal with the education of African American youngsters? What books/authors do you find who deal with African American contributions to U. S. society and history?
2. Oak Cliff Community Services Center (611 E. Jefferson): What type of social services does this organization provide to residents of Oak Cliff?
3. Video Potosino (608 E. Jefferson): What types of videos does this store feature? What videos do they have for children? How do they compare to the ones you normally rent?
4. Autobuses Avila Tours (608 A E. Jefferson, corner of Marsalis and Jefferson): What destinations does this company serve? How much is a one-way ticket to Matehuala? How often does a bus leave for San Miguel de Allende?
5. Autobuses Tornado (535 E. Jefferson): What are their major destinations in Mexico? How long is the trip? How often does the bus leave?
6. Pumpkin Patch Antiques (511 E. Jefferson): How do the items here compare with the other shop? Which ones interested you the most?
7. Transportes Rangel (501 E. Jefferson): What are their major destinations in Mexico? How long is the trip? How often does the bus leave? Do they go to the same destinations as Tornado?

INTERCULTURAL UNDERSTANDING

8. Los Sapitos Billar y Carambola (325 E. Jefferson): What type of game is carambola?
9. Oak Cliff Municipal Center (320 E. Jefferson): What offices are located in this building? Do any of them provide social services to residents of the area? Do any of them promote economic development in the area?
10. Super Mercado Monterrey (300 E. Jefferson): What items in the meat, fresh fruits and canned goods departments are different from those you have in your own local market? How do the prices on items similar to those found in your local market compare?
11. Panadería Espiga de Oro (303 E. Jefferson): What sorts of Guatemalan pastry and sweet breads did you find here? What, if any, special sweet breads do they prepare for Día de los Muertos or for Christmas? What type of bread is their specialty?
12. Dallas Inter-Tribal Center (209 E. Jefferson): What services does this organization offer to people in this area?

For lunch in this area try:

1. Panchita's Restaurant (720 E. Jefferson)
2. Valentino Chinese Restaurant (526 E. Jefferson)
3. Las Ranitas Restaurant (325 E. Jefferson)
4. Taquería Pedrito (321 E. Jefferson Blvd.)
5. El Regio (315 E. Jefferson Blvd.)
6. Sarai Restaurant (301 E. Jefferson)

After lunch, catch bus No. 510 "Sunset" (destination Hampton Station) back to the Cowart neighborhood. Get off at Searcy and walk west two blocks to the school.

INTERCULTURAL UNDERSTANDING

Appendix B

COMMUNITY PLUNGE

Objectives: This activity, a type of cultural scavenger hunt, is intended to provide interns with an introductory experience in the community served by the schools in which they will student teach. Through this activity, the interns will have the opportunity to identify and explore, in a limited fashion, several aspects of the community's socioeconomic and cultural organization. Additionally, the activity is intended to help interns begin to develop a spirit of camaraderie, which will be a useful support to them during their student teaching experience.

Activity Format: The interns will be divided into groups (four or five students per group). Each group will receive a map of the area, bus schedule, distinct route description, and a cultural questionnaire to be completed during the exploration of the particular route. Each group is to travel together on foot and by public transportation. Each group will have approximately three to four hours in which to conduct the community exploration. Prior to departure, group members will select one person for each of the following responsibilities:

    1. Tour Guide: knowing where all group members are at all times, helping group to decide which community elements to explore, keeping track of time

    2. Travel Agent: responsible for route directions, bus schedule, map, and helping group to decide where to explore

    3. Recorder: responsible for that data collected by group members is recorded on questionnaire

    4. Reporter: responsible for reporting salient findings/ observations to entire group during debriefing (NOTE: If the group has five members, then two Recorders may be selected.)

All groups will reassemble together to debrief the community plunge experience.

INTERCULTURAL UNDERSTANDING

YOU ARE ENCOURAGED TO UNDERTAKE THIS PLUNGE WITH SENSITIVITY, CREATIVITY, AND JOY TO GATHER INFORMATION AND INSIGHTS ABOUT YOUR NEW COMMUNITY.

HAVE FUN AND BE SAFE!

Appendix C

Community Plunge Debriefing Protocol

1. What problems did you encounter with your assigned route?
2. What city services, such as parks, did you observe?
3. What standards of beauty or taste did you experience (in terms of home adornment, clothing, cars, etc.)?
4. What evidence of social conflict did you see? (e.g. gang graffiti wars)
5. What evidence of wheel chair accessibility did you find on the sidewalks? restaurants? businesses?
6. What evidence of lack of code enforcement did you note?
7. What evidence of languages other than English did you find?
8. What types of social services did you investigate?
9. What types of businesses seemed to be predominant in the area?
10. What interesting places, not on the group questionnaire, did your group investigate?
11. How does this area compare to the area where you now live? What does it have that you do not and vice versa?
12. What was your most impressive or surprising finding or experience?

INTERCULTURAL UNDERSTANDING

13.   How did this experience alter your perception of Oak Cliff?
14.   What generalizations could you make about this community based on your immersion experience?
15.   What else could you do now to further explore your students' life and culture?
16.   As a teacher of students who live in this area, how would determine what prior knowledge or schema you must build so that your students can be successful in your class?
17.   What is one thing you experienced or saw that you could use in the classroom?

Collaboration to Foster Intercultural Understanding: The International Learning Community Model

Judi Repman
Cindi Chance
Stephanie Kenney
Pat Parsons
Georgia Southern University

Introduction

Teacher education institutions and public schools around the world face similar challenges with unfunded mandates: public accountability, evolving standards, increasingly stringent calls for higher performance with fewer resources, growing numbers of students with educational challenges, shrinking teaching forces, and the integration of technology. Suggesting that these forces can combine with changing student populations to form an imperative for change, A.F. Ball (2006) notes, "Globalization, technological advances, and the increasing number of students in classrooms worldwide who are from various racial, cultural, and linguistic backgrounds make multicultural and multilingual education an imperative in the 21st century" (p. 1). In 2001, the College of Education at Georgia Southern University partnered with five institutions in the United Kingdom (Cambridge University, University of Derby, University of East London, Sheffield Hallam University and Oxford Brookes University) to establish the International Learning Community (ILC). This paper describes the ILC response to these challenges, with particular attention given to how student teaching abroad opportunities can be used to foster a deeper understanding of diversity and awareness of intercultural issues. With its location in rural southeast Georgia, Georgia Southern University has long been aware of the need to provide ways for pre-service teachers to broaden their horizons to be better prepared to meet the needs of an increasingly diverse P-12 population in our service area.

Internationalizing teacher education

It isn't difficult to find American educational leaders who see the need for a new focus on internationalization within the teacher education curriculum. As David Imig and Joane McKay (2001) state so eloquently, "[T]here is the need to build global partnerships across national boundaries to address real problems that confront schools and school systems. Building these new connections is a major need and a way for learning organizations to thrive in the 21st century" (p. 10). There is little debate about the general lack of knowledge of American students when it comes to the rest of the world—in terms of basics such as geography, through more complex concepts such as language and culture. As the world shrinks and flattens as a result of economic and technological change, American students risk being left without the skills needed to be productive citizens in a global world (Ball, 2006; Heyl & McCarthy, 2003; Ling, Burman, Cooper, & Ling, 2006). Research (Cushner & Mahon, 2002; Heyl & McCarthy, 2003; Quezada, 2004) has shown that few pre-service teachers study a foreign language in college and even fewer participate in any kind of international experience, such as study abroad or student teaching in another country. The problem is not limited to pre-service teachers; in-service teachers and teacher educators need to participate in experiences that will allow them to infuse multicultural and international experiences into the teacher education curriculum (Ball, 2006; Heyl & McCarthy, 2003; Kelly, 2004; Merryfield, 2000; Merryfield, 2001). In its work with pre- and in-service teachers, the International Learning Community has consciously focused on providing ways to provide international, intercultural experiences. We concur with the idea that "teachers cannot teach what they do not know" (Sanders & Stewart, 2004, p. 204).

The United Kingdom faces many of the same challenges in preparing pre-service and in-service teachers. In 2005 the World Studies Trust published *Supporting the Standards: The Global Dimension in Initial Teacher Education and Training (ITET)*. This document includes a range of recommendations for stakeholders in the U.K. As part of the rationale for reframing the training of teachers to include a focus on internationalization, the Trust identified four areas of added value: motivation and retention, career enhancement, wider horizons, and participation and action (p. 3). These areas are extended into eight key concepts of the global dimension: global citizenship, conflict resolution, diversity, human rights, interdependence, social justice, sustainable development and values and perceptions (p. 4).

In a research project sponsored by a number of professional organizations, including the American Association of Colleges of Teacher Education (AACTE), Ann Schneider (2003) sought to answer the question, "What are the obstacles to increasing the international exposure of prospective teachers?" (p. 5). One critical finding supporting the need for a more active role by colleges of education relates to challenges faced when faculty and administrators work with campus international studies offices. Schneider's research found a lack of understanding about the roles and functions of international studies offices on the part of students, faculty, and staff in colleges of education. Interviews with international studies personnel found little knowledge of special factors related to study abroad by education students, such as the need for a network of cooperating teachers and other personnel to establish and oversee internships or student teaching experiences. Other recommendations center around the need to improve student advising and mentoring, reviewing the curriculum to increase focus on study of foreign languages, infusing international concepts in courses both inside and outside a college of education, and addressing challenges related to study abroad as part of the teacher education program of study. Schneider stresses the importance of early planning for education majors interested in an international experience, which requires that communication and collaboration between colleges of education and campus international study offices be efficient and effective.

Quezada (2004) notes that study abroad programs and an internationalized teacher education curriculum may not be the most effective way for pre-service teachers to gain the experiences needed to truly develop international knowledge and perspectives. Quezada states that most students involved in study abroad travel in groups, with a support system that insulates them from culture shock. The relative isolation and immersion of the student teaching experience, and the accompanying "out of place" feeling, is critical in developing deeper understanding of instructional pedagogy, learning about self, and genuine multiculturalism (p. 462). Thus, Quezada suggests that only by student teaching in another country can students "immerse themselves not only with the country but also within the schools and the community" (p. 458).

INTERCULTURAL UNDERSTANDING

Considerable research supports the value of actual experiences abroad in developing truly global educators. Cushner and Mahon (2002) studied fifty participants from the Consortium for Overseas Student Teaching. Analysis of responses from an open-ended questionnaire found significant improvements on students' beliefs about themselves and others and increased self-efficacy along with significant gains in global-mindedness and diversity. Research with teacher educators (Merryfield, 2000) found that effective global educators participated in "lived experiences" with individuals whose background and experiences differed significantly from the everyday lives of the teacher educators. Merryfield goes on to note that experiences alone are not enough. The experiences must lead to an on-going examination of self over time and across different cultural perspectives. Schneider (2003) also addresses the need for teacher education faculty development through workshops, travel abroad, and including international and foreign language competence in hiring and promotion.

Educational reform in the U.S. and the U.K.

Schools around the world are implementing various educational reforms. Parliaments, legislatures, and other policy making bodies have mandated a range of school improvement strategies. Although these programs may differ from one another in as many ways as the countries themselves do, they all have a common goal—to improve student learning.

The United Kingdom Parliament has approved a bill that closely mirrors the U.S. *No Child Left Behind (NCLB)* legislation. The *Improving the Quality of Education for All (IQEA)* project seeks to improve schools by both changing school culture and placing an emphasis on teaching and learning. *IQEA* attempts to concentrate change at the often overlooked classroom level (internal conditions), in addition to the school level, simultaneously. Societal changes, the failure of governments to base school policy on a research and/or knowledge base, the need for external and internal accountability agencies, and shared leadership are all additional issues addressed by proponents of policies in the U.S. and the U.K. Unfortunately, educational reform efforts in the United States have not included a significant focus on international education (Kelly, 2004). This means that it is left up to individual teacher training institutions and/or professional organizations to develop effective ways to promote cross-cultural approaches to address common critical issues (Kelly, 2004).

The International Learning Community response

Given these perspectives, and the imperative to attend to critical issues in rural, southeast Georgia, we began a dialog with our international partners that sought to 1) develop an understanding of, and respect for, teacher training models and school reform efforts in other countries; 2) envision teacher quality issues through international lenses; and 3) adopt and/or adapt tried and tested models into pre-service and in-service teacher professional development and teacher education faculty development. The result was the formation of the International Learning Community (ILC).

Both the U.S. and the U.K. spend millions of dollars/pounds on school improvement models. Shared resources and information can improve the efforts of both. Combining school and university resources from multiple sites to focus on applied research results in more efficient and effective models and promotes cross-cultural understanding and participation in the global society. All ILC members value global education as a way to "prepare young people to understand and interact within a culturally diverse and globally interconnected world" (Merryfield, quoted in Knighten, 2004, ¶4). We believe that international and intercultural education is closely related to teacher effectiveness and student achievement. Ball's research (2006) in the area of multicultural education supports the assertion and schools that effectively address and infuse multicultural education are more effective in terms of student learning and we believe that international education is a natural extension of multicultural education. Through a variety of ILC initiatives we have addressed common challenges and promoted shared goals. It is important to note from the outset that development of the ILC took place without additional external funding. Committed educators with a shared vision can follow a similar model to establish partnerships to address these and other issues of interest.

The five participating universities and their partner schools in the U.K. and the U.S. began the development of the ILC by identifying common challenges and have developed a shared comprehensive model and plan of action. With the ultimate goal of improving teaching and learning from pre-school through advanced education, the ILC's goals fall into five broad categories:

- Student/faculty professional development, including the development of intercultural perspectives and understandings;
- Curriculum development/renewal/alignment;
- Shared resources/expertise/curriculum;
- Collaborative research; and
- School improvement initiatives.

INTERCULTURAL UNDERSTANDING

To date, our most notable successes have come in terms of student/faculty professional development through exchange programs, shared resources/expertise/curriculum, and school improvement initiatives. Through our ILC involvement, Georgia Southern University has been invited to be a member of iNET, International Networking for Educational Transformation. iNET is an extension of the Specialist Schools and Academies Trust, a key component of U.K. educational reform. iNET holds conferences in locations around the world (including a conference hosted by Georgia Southern in 2006) to address school reform issues. The Specialist Schools and Academies Trust supports international efforts through the TIPD (Teachers' International Professional Development) Programme. Areas of focus for TIPD exchanges include raising standards, inclusion of special needs students, vocational education, turning around schools in challenging circumstances, effective use of technology, citizenship and civic education, and behavior management. The ILC mirrors the goals of the TIPD Programme since TIPD exchanges are limited to teachers in EU countries.

Initiatives related to student and faculty exchange have also begun under the auspices of the ILC. As discussed below, there are many challenges related to state rules regarding student teaching requirements, supervision and mentoring of student teachers, and funding for student teachers. All of the ILC partners continue to explore creative ways to address these challenges to increase opportunities for student and faculty exchanges. As Quezada (2004), Merryfield (2000, 2001), and others report, there is no substitute for actually spending time in another country/culture. Short-term faculty study tours, including school and university visits, have taken place in Georgia and the U.K. Special events such as the International Arts Academy, held in

INTERCULTURAL UNDERSTANDING

Statesboro in summer, 2006, have provided opportunities for K-12 student interaction. Georgia Southern has also displayed art work from U.K. students. Initial work is taking place to develop networks of researchers, with the ultimate goal of extending research opportunities to teacher educators seeking advanced degrees.

International student teaching

Twenty-one student teachers from Georgia Southern University have completed a portion of their student teaching in the U.K. since 2003 (ten early childhood majors, five special education majors, three middle grades majors, and four secondary education majors). As part of the debriefing from their experiences, students were asked to reflect not only on commonalities and differences in instruction, but also on their intercultural understandings. One student noted, "I will take knowing that all children are the same no matter where you go," a sentiment echoed by another student who stated that "I found that kids are kids no matter where they live or what language they speak. Teachers also have the same understanding and compassion for their students."

As faculty and staff from Georgia Southern have reviewed outcomes from sending student teachers to the U.K., we have attempted to provide our students with more opportunities to engage in critical reflection about their experiences. As a result, the six student teachers going to the U.K. in Spring, 2007 will be required to develop a portfolio including elements related to the four commitments in the College's conceptual framework. These include commitments to the knowledge, skills, and dispositions of the profession, to diversity, to technology and to the practice of continuous reflection and assessments. Artifacts and reflections related to diversity include approaches to working with special needs students, analysis of school diversity, reflection of teacher responses to diversity, and an examination of relevant standards in practice. We believe that creation of the portfolio will be instrumental in ensuring that the student teaching experience in the U.K. results in changed attitudes and new understandings of intercultural issues and the importance of global education.

Challenges and future directions

Initiatives such as the ILC can only go so far without additional funding and resources. Given the weakness of the U.S. dollar right now in the U.K., it has been a significant challenge to support student teachers who want to have an international experience. None of the ILC partners have access to free housing for student teachers, which also adds to the cost. Funding sources are also needed to support faculty exchanges and collaborative research.

Attitudinal challenges cannot be overlooked. Georgia Southern University is located in a conservative, rural area and not all of our constituents see the value of global education experiences or even an internationalized teacher education curriculum. Kelly (2004) notes that the emphasis on preparing teachers to work within the local community can also be a function of the kinds of institutions where many teacher preparation programs exist. Often only large research institutions have the resources to offer a wide range of areas studies programs. Area studies programs typically reach across campus colleges and departments, including faculty with specializations in related languages, history, anthropology, and literature. While area studies programs may exist apart from colleges of education, they can serve as a rich set of resources and contacts. Some faculty feel that there isn't any place in the curriculum for "new" content and we have found it challenging to engage them in a dialog about needed changes in curriculum and experiences (Bales, 2004; Heyl & McCarthy, 2003). Following the most recent terrorist attacks in London, two of our prospective student teachers decided they weren't comfortable with traveling and working abroad.

As noted above, state department of education and university rules make it a challenge to facilitate student teacher placements abroad. There are similar challenges for U.K. institutions who want to place student teachers in the U.S. We have found ways to work around these issues, but it takes time and energy to follow through.

As with many reform initiatives, continuity is an on-going challenge. The ILC began with a cohort of individuals (primarily university level teacher education faculty and administrators) who were deeply committed to developing a meaningful network addressing educational reform and student learning "across the pond." As individuals take on new jobs, retire, or move on to other tasks, it is critical to build an organization that isn't dependent on personalities. This is particularly important as the ILC works to increase the participation of our public school partners. We face challenges in communicating the benefits of ILC participation to a constantly changing group of teachers and administrators in our local public schools, which has major implications when it comes to planning productive exchanges of students and faculty. Fortunately, technology offers many opportunities to facilitate communication and disseminate information among ILC partners. We have already used video conferencing to conduct ILC meetings and plan to investigate other interactive technologies such as blogs as a way to increase communication.

Developing new degree programs and certificates is an area of interest to all ILC partners. With the addition of institutions from China to the partnership, we hope to be able to offer a doctoral degree that would allow students to study one summer in China, one summer in the U.K., and one summer in the U.S. While this degree is still very much in the discussion phase, we have begun planning for a graduate course and student exchange built on writing across the curriculum initiatives underway in participating countries.

As we have shared the benefits of ILC participation with other institutions, we hope to expand ILC membership. Adding a Chinese institution to the ILC builds on a Memorandum of Understanding in place at Georgia Southern University. With the growing importance of China and other Asian countries in the world economy and in world events, this partnership seems particularly critical. Expansion brings new challenges, but challenges keep the ILC a vital, growing learning community.

Implications

The challenges the ILC at Georgia Southern University has experienced are those typically found when developing an international initiative in a context in which internationalization of curriculum is a relatively new idea. These include lack of funding and infrastructure support, minimal faculty understanding of and dispositions toward international study curriculum, and curricular constraints between countries. These challenges suggest the following implications for the successful development and maintenance of any program such as our ILC:

- Institutional ILC funding support structure (through university and grant funding);
- Faculty dispositions toward international study (through inservice education and experience) ;
- International school and university curriculum map for ease of exchange (through ILC project);
- Institutionalization of the ILC concept (through integration into the curriculum); and
- Increased use of technology for ILC meetings and international course/program offerings (through school and university support at all ILC sites).

Conclusion

In its brief history, the ILC has experienced both the benefits and challenges of internationalizing our educator preparation curriculum. Through candidate and faculty exchanges, we have gained deeper understandings of the U.K. culture, its educational system, and its effective educational strategies aimed at meeting the learning needs of all learners. In addressing their field-based research questions about our educational system and culture, we have gained better insight into our own education system – its assumptions about diversity and the resulting effective/ineffective educational practices. We clearly see opportunities for expanding the ILC's activities more broadly in the U.K. and to other countries such as China. It is, however, important to first develop a strong foundation which will support the current and future development of the ILC.

INTERCULTURAL UNDERSTANDING

Resources

Improving the Quality of Education for All
http://www.iqea.com/
The International Learning Community
http://coe.georgiasouthern.edu/ilc/index.html
iNET (International Networking for Educational Transformation)
http://www.sst-inet.net/
Specialist Schools and Academies Trust
http://www.specialistschools.org.uk/

References

Bales, S.N. (2004). International education: Not a frill, and why not. *Phi Delta Kappan, 86,* 206-209.

Ball, A.F. (2006). *Multicultural strategies for education and social change: Carriers of the torch in the United States and South Africa.* New York: Teachers College Press.

Cushner, K., & Mahon, J. (2002). Overseas student teaching: Affecting personal, professional, and global competencies in an age of globalization. *Journal of Studies in International Education, 6*(1), 44-58.

Heyl, J.D., & McCarthy, J. (2003, January). International education and teacher preparation in the U.S. Paper presented at Global Challenges and U.S. Higher Education: National Needs and Policy Implications, Duke University. Available online at: http://www.internationaled.org/BriefingBook/4.EnhancingTeachers/4.c%20International.pdf

Imig, D.G., & McKay, J.W. (2001). Globalization and its implications for nations and peoples worldwide. Available online at: http://www.aacte.org/Programs/Global_International/DAVID.pdf

Kelly, J.A. (2004). Teaching the world: A new requirement for teacher preparation. *Phi Delta Kappan, 86,* 219-221.

Knighten, B. (2004). The importance of a global education: Interview with Dr. Merry Merryfield. Available online at: http://www.outreachworld.org/article.asp?articleid=77

Ling, L., Burman, E., Cooper, M., & Ling, P. (2006). (A)broad teacher education. *Theory into Practice, 45*(2), 143-149.

Merryfield, M.S. (2000). Why aren't teachers being prepared to teach for diversity, equity, and global interconnectedness? A study of lived experiences in the making of multicultural and global educators. *Teaching and Teacher Education, 16*, 429-443.

Merryfield, M.M. (2001, March). Implications of globalization for teacher education in the United States: Towards a framework for globally competent teacher educators. Paper presented at the First International Forum, AACTE 53rd Annual Meeting, Dallas, TX. Available online at: http://www.aacte.org/Programs/Global_International/MERRY.pdf

Quezada, R.L. (2004). Beyond educational tourism: Lessons learning while student teaching abroad. *International Education Journal, 5*(4), 458-465.

Sanders, T., & Stewart, V. (2004). International education: From community innovation to national policy. *Phi Delta Kappan, 86*, 200-205.

Schneider, A.I. (2003). *Internationalizing teacher education: What can be done? A research report on the undergraduate training of secondary school teachers.* Available online at: http://www.iienetwork.org/?p=44829

World Studies Trust. (2005). *Supporting the standards: The global dimension in initial teacher education and training.* Available online at: http://www.globalteacher.org.uk/global_dimension.htm

Influence of Background Experiences on the Support Needs of Alternatively Certified Novice Bilingual Teachers

Patricia Casey
Texas Woman's University
Michelle Abrego
University of Texas at Brownsville

As principals of neighboring elementary schools in a high-poverty urban area with large numbers of English language learners, we used to talk a lot about how to ensure that all of our bilingual students had strong teachers who could teach them what they needed to know to meet the demands of the high stakes tests that were lurking around every corner and, moreover, what they needed to know to be successful in life. The conversations often turned to a series of "how to's": how to find eligible candidates who could be certified as bilingual teachers to fill the many vacancies, how to ensure that such candidates would be competent teachers, how to retain the good bilingual teachers we had trained and how to best support the new bilingual teachers such that they could be effective from the first day. The challenge of attracting and retaining quality bilingual teachers was then, and still is, accentuated by a shortage of trained, licensed bilingual teachers and increased pressures for school accountability at both national and state levels. This finds confirmation in a National Academy of Education Committee on Teacher Education report which contends, "As a society, we do not invest seriously in the lives of children, most especially poor children and children of color, who receive the least-prepared teachers" (Darling-Hammond & Baratz-Snowden, 2007, p. 111). The Education Trust likewise reports that poor and minority students get more inexperienced teachers despite the knowledge that teacher effectiveness is the single biggest factor influencing gains in achievement (Haycock, 2004). Consequently, principals have to struggle to maintain a staff of qualified teachers willing to serve in urban schools (Jones & Sandige, 1997).

So, just as we did in our schools, many schools in urban areas are turning more frequently to a variety of alternative certification programs (ACP) to recruit teachers in high-need areas (Kwiatkowski, 1999). Information specifically related to the professional development needs of first year, alternatively certified teachers who begin their careers in high-poverty urban schools is limited. As the number of these teachers increases, it is imperative to examine how schools attempt to address their needs to become effective teachers. Earlier studies (Casey, 2004) suggest that novice, alternatively certified bilingual teachers may rely heavily on background experiences for support during the early years or that background experiences may mediate the strong need for support perceived by alternatively certified novice teachers. Thus, this paper presents a pilot study conducted to determine the manner in which background experiences impact alternatively certified teachers' support and capacity development needs.

Alternative teacher preparation programs vary in nature, scope and focus accentuating differences in teachers' readiness to teach. According to previous research, a main difference between traditional and alternative programs is that traditional certification programs attempt to prepare teachers for the schools we need whereas alternative certification programs try to prepare teachers for the schools we have (Hawley, 1992 as cited by Ovando & Trube, 2000). For this reason, alternatively certified teachers may tend to have different needs that require both structural and professional support, particularly during their first year of teaching.

Moreover, potential teachers differ in knowledge and skills before they start preparation programs. As noted by Darling-Hammond and Baratz-Snowden (2007):

> Some come steeped in their content area, but unfamiliar with children, curriculum, and schools. Others, while knowledgeable about child development, are ignorant about particular areas of content or instruction or classroom management. Still others have years of working with children or young adults in settings outside of schools—Sunday school, youth groups, and the like.... Some have a good sense of how to present information to students who learn easily in the way they teach, but lack the skills to reach students who learn in different ways, suffer gaps in their knowledge, or have particular learning difficulties. (p. 114)

A persistent shortage of bilingual teachers is most severe in elementary schools in urban areas where the most English language learners live (Barron & Menken, 2002). Increasing pressures for school accountability at both national and state levels coupled with federal mandates for highly qualified teachers in schools with high numbers of economically disadvantaged students accentuate the challenge of attracting and keeping quality teachers for high-poverty, urban schools. Bilingual teaching is considered a critical shortage area in states such as Texas where there is a large population of students for whom Spanish is their native language. The demands of this shortage of bilingual teachers have given rise to a number of non-traditional or alternative preparation programs.

These alternative programs are often developed to attract potential teachers to meet the needs of students in such areas of shortage. Alternative certification programs have increased the numbers of underrepresented minorities in the teaching force. According to the Education Commission of the States, "In Texas, 9% of all teachers are minorities and 41% of those who prepare through alternative routes are minorities" (Mikulecky, Shkodriani, & Wilner, 2004, p. 2). The diverse background experiences of the alternative certification candidates can contribute to the understandings or dispositions that teacher preparation programs seek to instill in potential teachers.

Hollins and Guzman (2005) argue that, unlike most potential teachers, minority candidates tend to have "social justice goals" and see themselves more "as change agents in the schools and in society." They further state that:

> The majority of teacher candidates are White, female, middle class, from suburbs or small towns, and have limited experience with those from cultures other than their own. Many candidates hold negative attitudes and beliefs about those different from themselves. Although many are willing to teach in urban areas despite lack of experience and skill, some are unwilling to teach in cities… Many candidates feel inadequately prepared to teach in urban areas. Candidates of color and their White counterparts have different experiences and different interests in teaching as a career. (p. 485)

According to Zumwalt and Craig (2005), "evidence is needed that demonstrates the contribution of a variety of factors including quality indicators that reflect the added value of teacher education programs, workplace context factors, teacher dispositions and personality traits" (p. 187). Learning to teach requires understanding of students and social contexts as well as knowledge of content and pedagogical skills. Darling-Hammond and Baratz-Snowden (2007) note:

INTERCULTURAL UNDERSTANDING

In addition to knowledge that is connected to tools and practices, teachers need to develop a set of dispositions—or habits of thinking and action—about teaching, children, and the role of the teacher. These include the disposition to reflect and to learn from practice; a willingness to take responsibility for children's learning; determination and persistence in working with children until they succeed; the will to continue to see new approaches to teaching that will allow greater success with students. (p. 122)

So, even though alternative certification programs may expedite training in content and pedagogical skills, the candidates' background experiences may serve, in contrast, to enhance these essential understandings and dispositions about students and social contexts.

Recent research has questioned and evaluated the effectiveness of both traditional and alternative teacher preparation programs (Goldhaber & Brewer, 2001), and suggested additional exploration of the demands imposed on new teachers, particularly those from alternative paths. (Darling-Hammond, Berry, & Thoreson, 2001). While most of the literature about alternative certification candidates focuses on discrete variables such as race, gender, ethnicity, and test scores, Chin and Young (2007) developed a more holistic, ecological model of development that focuses on "persons and situates their desires and attitudes toward teaching as shaped by their particular life circumstances and personal histories"(p. 74). Similarly, this pilot study was developed to increase our understanding of how the support needs of beginning teachers from alternative certification programs were influenced by their personal background experiences.

Study purpose and methods

The purpose of this pilot study was to determine the perceptions of alternatively certified bilingual teachers serving in high-poverty urban elementary schools. Based on the literature, the study was developed to focus on three areas: a) the participants' perceptions of relevant personal background experiences, b) the support and professional growth needs of these teachers, and c) the actual work experiences of these teachers in high-poverty urban elementary schools.

The purpose was to identify phenomena through the perceptions of the teachers themselves in this particular situation (Taylor & Bogdan, 1984), and to focus on how they interpreted their experiences and the meaning of those experiences (Van Manen, 1990; Merriam, 1998). According to Merriam (1998), the sample in a qualitative study is typically purposefully selected, not random, and small. To this end, surveys were collected from 12 alternatively certified bilingual teachers who are novice teachers with one to three years of experience. As a result, these data may not be generalizable, but they do offer some suggestions for further research.

This study employed survey data from a questionnaire that was developed for preliminary data collection with both closed ended, quantitative type questions and open ended, qualitative type questions. Two sources of data are included in this study. The first part of the survey and source of data includes closed ended questions designed to provide demographic and background information about the participants. The second source of data is from the open ended questions and provides individual and foundational information about their perceptions of the support they needed and received. The researchers attempted to focus on teachers' experiences in order to develop an in-depth understanding of each case. These data were analyzed inductively to capture emerging themes. As such, every line of the responses from the open ended questions was coded and these codes were organized by categories to look for patterns or themes (Lincoln & Guba, 1985; Patton, 2002; Miles & Huberman, 1994).

Findings

The findings from this pilot study are discussed according to the three areas of focus. These include a) background experiences, b) support needs of alternatively certified bilingual teachers, and c) their actual work experiences in high-poverty urban elementary schools.

Background experiences

Demographic information. According to Zumwalt and Craig (2005), most teachers are female, White and monolingual. In contrast, these respondents had very diverse backgrounds and life experiences. Ten of the respondents were female and two were male. Ages ranged from 20 to 41 years old, 3 were single and the other 9 were married. Of the respondents, 7 were Hispanic and 5 were White. All were bilingual (Spanish/English) and bi-literate as required by their position as a bilingual teacher. These data describe a population different from the teaching force as a whole.

Academic training. Researchers continue to debate the effectiveness of using a degree from an accredited university in teaching, GPA, tests of verbal ability, or subject matter expertise as a proxy for teacher quality (Zumwalt & Craig, 2005). The evidence supporting each is inconclusive. All of these respondents had bachelor's degrees and 3 had master's degrees in fields other than education. As elementary generalists, they taught all subject areas, so it would have been cumbersome to test subject matter knowledge. However, it should be noted that one respondent reported the spending of extra time and effort to learn the academic content as an obstacle in her first year of teaching.

The respondents' degrees represented academic training in several areas such as social psychology, marketing, business administration, anthropology, Spanish, English, communications, and global studies. One reported that the duration of the alternative certification program (ACP) was 3 months (clearly not including the year of teaching required by the state for certification); the others reported 1, 1.5 or 2 years in the ACP. At the time of the survey, all were teaching in public elementary schools—Pre-kindergarten through 4th grade—except one who was teaching in a private preschool.

Work experiences. Background experiences that may mediate the strong support needs for novice teachers emerged from the data in several areas. The respondents reported very diverse work experiences prior to entering the ACP. For example, 3 of the respondents were in business/marketing, 2 were in social work, one was in the military, one was a stay-at-home mom, and one was unemployed.

The respondents referred to work-related experiences as relevant to their success in teaching. First, a high number (75%) of the participants reported some experience in their backgrounds with teaching such as volunteer or paid tutoring; training, tutoring or supervising children in orphanages/church schools/non-profits; or training adults related to business or social services. Two of the respondents were working in the corporate world as trainers. And two were working in private preschools while one was teaching

English to adults in a private school. This experience may lead to an increased sense of self-efficacy and, consequently, a decreased need for psychological support.

From their work and life experiences, several of the respondents also referred to having developed personal skills such as patience, organizational skills, interpersonal communication skills and/or time management skills that were very helpful to them in their new careers as teachers. One teacher mentioned having learned, in addition, "a good work ethic" just as others talked about relying on a "strong work ethic," feeling responsible and making a contribution. And they referred to having developed useful business skills by coordinating or managing complex projects and/or owning and managing their own businesses.

Additionally, some of the respondents drew on other life experiences that they had prior to entering teaching. Their experiences with social and cultural diversity seemed to prepare them in a unique way for the challenges of teaching in the diverse, urban setting in which they were now working. For example, one teacher said, "I grew up in a very diverse city and lived in different states, and I think this helped me adjust to the different personalities, values and cultures that people possess."

These experiences with diverse cultures may mediate some of the stress that new teachers experience. Consistent with Hollins and Guzman's (2005) idea that many teachers feel unprepared to work in urban schools, other authors (Ryan, 1970; Veenman, 1984) found that new teachers face a "reality shock" or "culture shock" when they encounter the realities of classroom life. The socialization into the profession begins in the first year of teaching but continues for several years thereafter (Brock & Grady, 2001). The context or sociological setting varies between schools, and beginning teachers are expected to apply general knowledge that would normally be obtained from preparation programs to teaching in diverse school settings and working with diverse student populations.

The alternative certification programs

Interestingly, the reasons given by the respondents for deciding to pursue teacher certification varied considerably. Only two of the respondents expressed a sense of calling to "serve society" or "help people" and three referred to the benefits of teaching as a career such as more "time with my family" or that they "would always have a job" or "something to fall back on." More than half of the respondents (7) described a "need for a change" or being "at a crossroads in my life" and referred to responding to an opportunity that presented itself. Although these respondents welcomed the opportunity to become certified, they also said that they wanted to be teachers, and it was not just a matter of needing a job. Earlier research noted that there are "differences in career changers who enter alternative teacher preparation programs based on a desire to teach as compared with those career changers entering motivated by necessity—they need a job... Career changers who were successful in their previous careers are much more likely to bring that success to the classroom" (Hayes, 2005, p. 162).

Respondents gave three reasons for choosing the ACP rather than traditional university preparation programs. One said that the ACP was more accessible and that it was too difficult to get information from the university-based program to even see if she was interested. One said that she chose the program because it was highly recommended by a friend. Significantly, each of the respondents (100%) said that he or she chose the ACP because it was faster. Most expressed that they did not feel a need to do the university course work for a second bachelor's degree, and that they did not see the point or purpose of doing so. They were already in the workforce and unwilling or unable to give up their regular income to participate in a traditional university preparation program. One said, "If you have the option of an alternative certification, what is the point of going to college and spending that amount of years?" Another added, "the cost and commitment of attending college… was too much to consider at the time.

In-service support and professional growth needs

Support needs

The respondents reported that they faced many obstacles during their first year of teaching. Most salient among these obstacles were:
- lack of important information about procedures and responsibilities;
- not having an experienced teacher or mentor to help with or model lessons;
- lack of time to plan and prepare; high volumes of paperwork;
- not knowing how to teach (pedagogical skills);
- lack of parent involvement;
- lack of support from grade level team; and
- difficulty with student/classroom management.

These obstacles correspond with earlier studies which show the support needs for alternatively certified bilingual teachers such as personal and collegial interactions, additional pre-service experiences, technical information about school operations and curriculum, and more time to reduce the stress level associated with an overwhelming initial year of teaching (Casey, 2004).

INTERCULTURAL UNDERSTANDING

The reported obstacles by our respondents are consistent with the challenges identified by beginning teachers in the MetLife Survey of the American Teacher (2005). New teachers reported their biggest challenges as communicating with and involving parents (33%), difficulty in obtaining sufficient classroom resources (22%), and overall problems in maintaining classroom discipline and management (20%). Furthermore, new teachers also reported challenges related to the level of collegial support. Lack of support included not being assigned a more experienced teacher as a mentor (19%), having no one to go to for guidance in teaching the curriculum (12%), classroom management (9%), and administrative responsibilities (9%).

While the respondents chose the ACP because it was, as one articulated, "quicker and cheaper," some of the biggest challenges that the respondents faced in their first years of teaching may have related directly to the corresponding lack of knowledge or field experiences prior to teaching. This is consistent with findings from earlier research (Hayes, 2005) that the program duration may have an impact on teacher performance.

It was anticipated that certain career, social or personal background experiences might influence the novice teachers' perceptions of these needs. The respondents recognized that there were things they needed to know that perhaps they might have learned in a more extensive preparation program. One expressed that the ACP "didn't explain a lot of procedures in detail." Further, respondents mentioned not knowing enough about a) how to differentiate instruction to meet the varied needs of diverse learners, b) how to use resources/curriculum materials, c) effective classroom management/student discipline, d) parent involvement/parent conferences, and e) managing time, paperwork, and administrative requirements. Some also mentioned the need for more pre-service or in-service field experiences (most had two or three weeks of student teaching in summer school and few additional observation times with other teachers).

Supportive people and strategies

Eleven of the 12 respondents named other *people* when asked, "*What* contributed the most to your success as a teacher?" Among those named were grade level teams, school staff/co-workers, school administrators, mentors, and families. In contrast, some of the same categories of people were mentioned by more than a few of the respondents as being of very little help or, in fact, obstacles to success. In those situations, respondents named other sources of help, which may be indicative of their initiative or persistence. One mentioned the ACP training and the field support provided by the ACP. Another mentioned a new teacher academy that was a formal induction program for new teachers provided by the district.

Recognizing the obstacles they faced, the respondents each reported how and from whom they received needed support. Most of the respondents reported feeling they were "still a work-in-progress" but they recalled drawing on personal skills such as creativity, patience and willingness to initiate conversations and ask for what they needed. One said, "Being self-reliant by nature, I read a lot, asked a lot of questions. I believe I drove two teacher friends crazy." Some of the participants said that they simply "worked hard," drawing on their personal work ethic.

The respondents who did not perceive the assigned mentor, grade level teams or other colleagues to be helpful reported taking the initiative to seek help from friends, neighbors, family, ACP cohort members, other teachers, or other school staff. In these cases, the novice teachers' initiative, persistence, or tenacity was instrumental in his/her success. Consistent with earlier research (Haberman, 1995), persistence is an attribute of effective teachers for children in poverty. Moreover, this insight may indicate that these teachers would benefit from a support team involving people from the ACP and a wider range of school staff.

Additionally, several of the teachers also articulated having struggled with self-confidence but drawing on personal strengths and persistence to meet that challenge. For example, one stated, she had to relax her "own expectations for herself." Another said, "I learned not to dwell on shortcomings but focus on my strengths." A third reported, "I had to develop more confidence in myself and my teaching." She continued by saying how she deliberately worked on it. This characteristic described as persistence or tenacity in the literature is recognized as a predictor of success for ACP teachers (USDE, 2004). It is also noted that resiliency has been identified as a trait shared by teachers who remained in the profession (Bobek, 2002).

Two of the respondents said that in-service professional development workshops had helped them. But, interestingly, one of them said that the workshop had helped her because at the workshop she met an experienced teacher who had given her advice and support. The other referred to the skills learned in the workshop as being helpful.

Experiences in high-poverty urban elementary schools

It was anticipated that teachers who enter teaching as career changers, who express dissatisfaction with a prior career, or who enter teaching with strong ties to the community, would affirm a strong personal sense of calling. Correspondingly, a strong personal sense of calling to teaching and sense of dedication to their students emerged from the data. (Although only two respondents originally indicated a sense of calling as their original reason for entering an ACP, most indicated they had always wanted to be teachers). These teachers reported caring deeply about their students and recognizing their opportunity to help their students or to serve as a role model for their students. This finding is consistent with earlier studies revealing that alternatively certified bilingual teachers experience a strong personal sense of calling to teaching and dedication to their students (Casey, 2004) and Hollins and Guzman's (2005) idea that minority teachers may be more committed to social justice and serving as a change agent in society. Respondents articulated this sense of calling repeatedly.

Valenzuela (1999, p. 266) further argues for an "authentically caring pedagogy" to enhance students' cultural identities, build social capital and reverse the negative effects of what she calls "subtractive schooling." Thus, the caring pedagogy and cultural connection enhances the alternatively certified teachers' effectiveness. One said, "…I love what I'm doing and I feel complete. There is not a single day when I regret being a teacher. I love my job."

Conclusions and recommendations

Alternative teacher certification has gained attention and recognition as one avenue to respond to the current demand for more qualified teachers, particularly in strong areas of need like bilingual education. While much has been written about the provision of induction support during the first three years of teaching, little research casts light on how induction support might differ for alternatively certified novice teachers (Darling-Hammond et al., 2001; Goldhaber & Brewer, 2001; Ovando &

Trube, 2000). Therefore, instructional leaders must search for innovative ways to enhance the teaching capacity of alternatively certified bilingual teachers so that all students may indeed experience academic success. Thus, this study attempts to determine the impact of the novice bilingual teachers' background experiences on their support and professional growth needs.

Recommendations for educational leaders

Principals and other school leaders may benefit from the findings of this study to enhance hiring practices and planning for induction support and/or ongoing professional development for new bilingual teachers. These findings may suggest that alternatively certified bilingual teachers have different support and professional growth needs because they enter teaching through different life and career paths. These varied background experiences influenced the teachers' needs both positively and negatively. Given that alternatively certified bilingual teachers will likely begin their careers in high-poverty urban schools that serve large numbers of English language learners, principals who hire these teachers may benefit from increased awareness of how their personal background experiences can influence their support needs.

These findings also suggest that support needs may be increased because of the expedited training coupled with the high-need school setting. These teachers felt they had less pre-service training and needed more help in areas such as pedagogical skills, student discipline, and managing time and curricula. Additionally, a number of social factors associated with poverty and cultural and linguistic differences of the student population made the bilingual classrooms even more challenging than most. Poverty is, for example, associated with less access to formal learning, fewer resources, greater health problems, and greater incidence of developmental delays (Garcia, 2001). Given the increased stress and workload associated with the student demographics, alternatively certified, bilingual teachers in high-poverty schools may require a great deal of additional support than is typically offered.

Our ACP teachers shared many of the overall concerns of beginning teachers regardless of their certification route (traditional or ACP). However, of particular importance for school administrators is the need to provide additional pedagogical support to bilingual ACP teachers. Our respondents identified *not knowing how to teach* as an obstacle. Additionally, the second most frequently noted impediment for beginning teachers in the MetLife American Teacher Survey (2005)—sufficient resources—was not identified as an obstacle for our teachers. A lack of teaching resources in Spanish is commonly cited as a major concern for bilingual teachers in the literature (Banks, 1989). Thus, the bilingual ACP teachers may have a particular need for strong support in the identification of proper resources and teaching strategies beyond that of other beginning teachers.

On the other hand, while the teachers may have needed more support with such job specific tasks as lesson planning or pedagogical skills due to their expedited pre-service training, they reported having a wealth of knowledge from prior work experiences—job skills such as organization and communication. And the findings suggest that novice teachers who have experience working in the schools or other relevant work/life experiences may need less psychological support due to increased feelings of self-efficacy that lessen the high stress and self-doubt characteristic of new teachers.

The findings may also indicate that alternatively certified bilingual teachers experience a strong sense of calling to teaching in high-need schools. Unlike the typical teacher described earlier by Hollins and Guzman (2005), the alternatively certified teachers are more likely to be teachers of color and more likely to enter teaching after experiencing a lack of fulfillment in another career. Therefore, they may feel a particularly strong sense of reward, commitment to the students, and/or dedication to the profession. Those who enter teaching with a background in the community may also feel even stronger ties to the community and accentuated commitment to the students. In this manner, the novice teacher's cultural background and life experiences in the community may also alleviate the cultural dissonance that can occur between novice teachers and their bilingual students in high-poverty urban schools.

Alternative certification programs are known for capitalizing on candidates' background experiences. Such is the case when beginning teachers are accepted in an alternative certification program specifically because of their bilingualism, maturity, and accumulated work experience (Stoddart & Floden, 1995). Alternatively certified teachers may need more and differentiated in-service training and support that is focused on their assignment and the context in which they are teaching. Teachers in fast-moving alternative certification programs may benefit from additional support in the form of reduced responsibilities at work or extended time to complete assignments in order to make the most of in-service training.

Recommendations for teachers or prospective teachers

One of the survey respondents offered suggestions to "provide students with teachers who are not only highly qualified but also

INTERCULTURAL UNDERSTANDING

highly confident." Another said, "From my limited experience, I have decided that alternatively-certified teachers seem to be more willing to implement new instructional strategies, seem more reflective on their teaching practices, and more willing to collaborate." The following suggestions were offered by the teachers who responded to this pilot survey for other novice teachers from ACP or for people who are considering entering alternative certification programs.

- Ask lots of questions, be assertive, do not be afraid to ask.
- Be ready and willing to work hard. Be prepared to work long hours. Be realistic about teacher hours, stress of high stakes testing and paperwork. "I love my job, which feels more like my second home. But like any home (filled with kids) the work is <u>never, ever</u> done."
- Make sure you have the full support of your family because the first year of teaching is not easy. But it's all necessary and worth it in the end—there are lessons you can only learn by going through them yourself. And the kids make it all worth it.
- Observe other teachers, visit schools, volunteer whenever possible—spend time working with students before you start the program to be sure teaching is good match.
- Read as much as you can about teaching.
- Look for a good principal. Look for a good district. Look for a good mentor.
- Seek out more training on classroom management.
- Accept chaos not only in your classroom but emotionally. Know that most of us do one day at a time. Be kind to yourself.
- Remember that this is a noble profession that benefits children.

Final thoughts

Although this study focused on a very small number of alternatively certified bilingual teachers, the study of individual cases such as these sheds some light on the somewhat obscure subject of the support needs of these teachers. More research is needed.

There is substantial evidence that alternative certification programs open doors for more aspiring teachers from underrepresented groups. This alone is reason to hope that one day the face of our teaching force will look more like the faces of our students, eliminating the cultural dissonance so many new teachers fear and feel in high-poverty urban schools.

The data demonstrate that the participating teachers brought with them to the profession an ethic of caring and a desire to serve society. They brought job skills and a strong work ethic. They asked for help and information that they needed. They persisted in spite of obstacles because they cared about children and because they believed in teaching as a profession.

References

Banks, S. (1989, November 21). Schools are frustrated by bilingual demands. *Los Angeles Times*, pp. A1, A 24.

Barron, V., & Menken, K. (2002). What are the characteristics of the bilingual education and ESL teacher shortage? Washington, DC: National Clearinghouse for English Language Acquisition & Language Instruction Educational Programs. Retrieved March 28, 2005 from http://www.ncela.Gwu.edu/expert/faq/14shortage.htm

Bobek, B. (2002). Teacher resiliency: A key to career longevity. *Clearing House, 75*, (4), 202-205.

Brock, B. L., & Grady, M. L. (2001). *From first year to first rate: Principals guiding beginning teachers.* Thousand Oaks, CA: Corwin Press.

Casey, P.J. (2004). Providing support for first year alternatively certified bilingual teachers in high-poverty urban elementary schools. Unpublished dissertation, University of Texas at Austin.

Chin, E., & Young, J. (2007). A person-oriented approach to characterizing beginning teachers in alternative certification programs. *Educational Researcher. 36*(2) pp. 74-83.

Darling-Hammond, L., Berry, B., & Thoreson, A. (2001). Does teacher certification matter? Evaluating the evidence. *Educational Evaluation and Policy Analysis. 23*(1), pp. 57-77.

Darling-Hammond, L., & Baratz-Snowden, J. (2007, Winter). A good teacher in every classroom: Preparing the highly qualified teachers our children deserve. *Educational Horizons, 85*(2), pp. 111-132.

Garcia, E. E. (2001). *Hispanic education in the United States: Raices y alas.* Boulder, CO: Rowman & Littlefield.

Goldhaber, D., & Brewer, D. (2001). Evaluating the evidence on teacher certification: A rejoinder. *Educational Evaluation and Policy Analysis, 23*(1), pp. 79-86.

Haberman, M. (1995). *Star teachers of children in poverty.* West Lafayette, IN: Kappa Delta Pi.

Haycock, K. (2004). The real value of teachers: If good teachers matter, why don't we act like it? *Thinking K-16, 8* (1), pp. 1-44. Retrieved from http://www2.edtrust.org/NR/rdonlyres/B58863F7-B15D-4E7C-82DE-08CFFD867774/0/TNpk162007.ppt #1518,59,Poor and Minority Students Get More Inexperienced* Teachers

Hayes, J. (2005). Overview and framework: Alternative certification teacher preparation programs: Effects of program models on teacher performance. In J.R. Dangel &

E.M.Guyton (Eds.), *Research on alternative and non-traditional education: Teacher education yearbook XIII* (pp.81-90). Lanham, MD: Association of Teacher Educators with Rowman & Littlefield Publishing Group.

Hollins, E.R., & Guzman, M.T. (2005). Research on preparing teachers for diverse populations. In M. Cochran-Smith & K. Zeichner (Eds.), *Studying teacher education: The report of the AERA panel on research and teacher education* (pp.477-548). Mahwah, NJ: Lawrence Erlbaum.

Jones, D., & Sandidge, R. F. (1997), Recruiting and retaining teachers in urban schools: Implications for policy and the law. *Education and Urban Society, 29*(2), 192-204.

Kwiatkowski, M. (1999). Debating alternative teacher certification: A trial by achievement. In M. Kanstoroom & C. E. Finn, Jr. (Eds.), *Better teachers, better schools* (pp. 215–238). Washington, DC: Thomas B. Fordham Foundation. Retrieved from at http://www.edexcellence.net/better/tchrs/15.htm

Lincoln, Y. S., & Guba, E. G. (1985). *Naturalistic inquiry.* Beverly Hills, CA: Sage.

Merriam, S. B. (1998). *Qualitative research and case study applications in education.* San Francisco: Jossey-Bass.

MetLife. (2005). *MetLife's survey of the American teacher: Transitions and the role of supportive relationships 2004-2005.* Retrieved April 16, 2007, from http://www.metlife.com/WPSAssets/34996838801118758796V1FATS_2004.pdf.

Mikulecky, M., Shkodriani, G., & Wilner, A. (2004, December). A growing trend to address the teacher shortage. *Policy Brief: Alternative Certification.* Denver, CO: Education Commission of the States. Retrieved April 16, 2007 from http://www.ecs.org/html/educationIssues/StateNotes/2004_PolicyBrief_Collection.pdf

Miles, M.B., & Huberman, A. M. (1994). *Qualitative data analysis* (2nd ed.). Thousand Oaks, CA: Sage.

Ovando, M. N., & Trube, B. (2000, July). Capacity building of beginning teachers from alternative certification programs: Implications for instructional leadership. *Journal of School Leadership, 10,* 346-366.

Patton, M. Q. (2002). *Qualitative research and evaluation methods.* Thousand Oaks, CA: Sage.

Ryan, K. (Ed.). (1970). *Don't smile until Christmas.* Chicago: University of Chicago Press.

Stoddart, T., & Floden, R. E. (1995). *Traditional and alternative routes to teacher certification: Issues, assumptions, and misconceptions.* East Lansing, MI: National Center for Research on Teaching.

Taylor, S. J., & Bogdan, R. (1984). *Introduction to qualitative research methods: Search for meaning* (2nd ed.) New York: John Wiley.

United States Department of Education Office of Innovation and Improvement. *Alternative routes to teacher certification.* Washington, DC: Author.

Valenzuela, A. (1999). *Subtractive schooling: U.S.-Mexican youth and the politics of caring.* Albany: State University of New York.

Van Manen, M. (1990). *Researching lived experiences: Human science and action sensitive pedagogy.* New York: State University of New York Press.

Veenman, S. (1984). Perceived problems of beginning teachers. *Review of Educational Research, 54*(2), 143-178.

Zumwalt, K., & Craig, E. (2005). Teachers' characteristics: Research on the indicators of quality. In M. Cochran-Smith & K. Zeichner (Eds.), *Studying teacher education: The report of the AERA panel on research and teacher education* (pp.157-260). Mahwah, NJ: Lawrence Erlbaum Associates, Publishers.

Braiding Cultural Understandings: Reflections of a Teacher Working with Diverse Latino Parents

Patsy J. Robles-Goodwin
Texas Wesleyan University

Introduction

Strong parental involvement in a child's education and school environment has shown to be essential to the success of the child and the school. Effective parental involvement is an individualized, comprehensive, purposeful, and ongoing process designed to ensure that all parents are connected to the school's culture, purpose, and organization. La Roche and Shriberg (2004) report that high parental school involvement and parenting practices are two family variables shown to have the greatest impact on academic achievement among families of different ethnicities and socioeconomic levels. However, meaningful parental involvement has traditionally eluded schools because school norms and structures have historically been, and to a large part continue to be, most responsive to parents who are middle-class, U.S.- born, and standard-English-speaking individuals (King & Goodwin, 2002; Jiménez, 2002). Although these norms seem firmly well established in most schools, there is an urgent need for schools to become more inclusive of diverse populations as the nation's demographics continue to change.

With increasing numbers of linguistically and culturally diverse students, our schools are faced with the task of serving students and families with limited English skills. Teachers are challenged with developing effective educational and literacy programs to include the cultural and linguistic diversity of the student population (August, 2006; Prince & Lawrence, 1993; Valencia 2002).

Recently, Latino students have attracted the attention of educators, legislators, and the public in general because Latinos now constitute the largest group of minority students in many U.S. schools, especially in urban areas. Latinos experienced a 59 percent growth rate during the 1990s (Jiménez, 2002). Latino immigrant families also are more likely to live in poverty as compared to other ethnic groups (Capps, Fix, & Reardon-Anderson, 2003). In 2000, the poverty rate for Latinos was 22.5%, compared to 7.7% for non-Hispanic Whites (U.S. Census Bureau, 2001). Research in the area of poverty indicates children and families living in poverty learn unique ways to cope and survive in their situation creating the equivalent of a new culture (Chafel, 1997; Chall, Jacobs, & Baldwin, 1990; Jalango, 1996; McLoyd, 1995). Therefore, teachers may need to be equipped with specific knowledge about working with diverse Latino families, coupled with ways to work with Latino families that may also be living in poverty. With growth rates of Latinos predicted to continue increasing in the future, schools are being challenged to strengthen school-home connections and utilize best practices to increase the academic achievements of Latino students who may also be living in poverty (Klein & Chen, 2001; Lynch & Hanson, 2004).

Where do teachers learn how to develop these specialized programs for diverse students? In many of the traditional multicultural classes for undergraduates, differences between the cultures are studied in an attempt to better understand their nuances. However, the problem with this approach is that the undergraduate pre-service teachers may learn stereotypes or cultural nuances of the ethnic groups, believing individuals within that group are homogeneous in their lifestyles, beliefs, or values. This approach causes confusion when working with diverse student populations in a school setting. In fact, many ethnic groups have many cultural similarities among them, but there are still many differences, especially when working with Latino parents (Nieto, 2004).

This article makes a case for improving the school success of diverse Latino students through the framework of culturally responsive teaching and preparing educators with the knowledge, attitudes, and skills needed to accomplish this goal. The ideas presented here are brief scenarios that have occurred throughout the author's professional experiences in working with Latino families as a teacher and researcher. A case is made for interacting with Latino families in a variety of ways in order to incorporate the student's culture into the curriculum.

This article also addresses culturally biased beliefs many educators may have toward their Latino students and families, as well as a variety of ways schools and parents can work together for the benefit of the students. The goal is for administrators, parents, prospective teachers, and teacher educators to develop an understanding of culturally responsive parental involvement as it relates to working with diverse Latinos.

Gay's (2000) five essential elements of culturally responsive teaching are used as a framework for beginning a paradigm shift: (1) developing a knowledge base about cultural diversity, (2) including ethnic and cultural diversity content in the curriculum, (3) demonstrating caring and building learning communities, (4) communicating with diverse students, and (5) responding to ethnic diversity in the delivery of instruction. For the purposes of this article, the term "culturally responsive" is used because it acknowledges that all families have varied backgrounds, beliefs, and values. The families are evolving, complex, and ever-changing, but they recognize the need to be involved in their children's schools (King & Goodwin, 2002).

Culturally responsive teaching is defined as using the cultural characteristics, experiences, and perspectives of diverse students as a way for teaching them more effectively. When academic knowledge and skills are derived from the experiences and frames of reference of students, they are more personally meaningful, interesting, and are learned easily (Gay, 2000). As a result, the academic achievement of ethnically diverse students, in particular Latinos, will improve when they are taught using their cultural and experiential filters (Au & Kawakami, 1994; Gay, 2000; Hollins, 1996; Ladson-Billings, 1995).

Culturally responsive teaching

Culture can be defined as all aspects of life that influence our thinking and our behavior. Specific facets of culture can include language, education, age, gender, religion, geography, time, health, proximal space, social economic status, and values. Cultural groups differ with respect to values, education, language, roles of family members, problem-solving strategies, views of life and death, attitudes toward education, health, and level of commitment to traditional or nontraditional ways (Okagaki & Diamond, 2000; Klein & Chen, 2001).

The lack of awareness of these differences among Latino families may lead to miscommunications and misunderstandings resulting in unintentional stereotyping in a school setting. Therefore, specific cultural sensitivity and knowledge is essential for providing effective schooling to Latino students, even if the classroom teacher is from the Latino group. In other words, many Latino teachers may be able to identify with many of the cultural aspects of the Latino culture. However, there may also be areas in which the cultural norm of Latino families may be completely different than the experiences of the Latino teacher due to the teacher's socioeconomic status affecting educational background, Spanish proficiency and literacy, foods and geography—different parts of the U.S., including urban, suburban, and rural areas (Zainuddin, Yahya, Morales-Jones, & Ariza, 2002).

For example, many teachers assume that all Latinos share the same religious beliefs and faith. While many Latinos follow Catholic teachings, they are very diverse in their beliefs. One mother informed me in early December that her religion did not allow for her and the family to celebrate any holidays, including birthdays. Therefore, she asked that I not allow her daughter to participate in the upcoming holiday party. While I had not ever been asked to do this, I felt it was inappropriate in regard to the child's feelings. After all, she would be watching while her classmates played games and ate party foods. I did not feel the student would understand all the implications at her young age. I requested the mother simply pick her daughter up early that day. Because of work commitments, she stated it would not be possible. I then proposed the option of sending her to another classroom with the music teacher. I knew this teacher did not have a homeroom class during our party time. The music teacher and my student ended up playing checkers while the majority of the students participated in their parties. I often think of this situation, and felt I handled it as respectfully as possible. In my years as a classroom teacher, this type of request from Latino parents only increased. The only difference is I now have had the time to reflect on the situation and to offer some options that acknowledge the parents' requests, while still considering the emotions of the students.

As a researcher, I observed a classroom in which a handful of kindergarten Spanish-speaking students were interacting with a monolingual English-speaking teacher. She was an excellent and experienced teacher with an advanced degree who enjoyed working with English language learners (ELLs). The students were learning to speak English, but still only communicated with their teacher using a beginning level English vocabulary. They were trying to explain to the teacher that one of the students had lost a tooth and that the "Raton" (Rat) would visit and take the tooth in exchange for some money. (This tradition is very similar to the tooth fairy experience in American culture). The teacher did not understand this cultural tradition and could not connect with the students' cultural experiences, and the students did not have enough English vocabulary skills to inform the teacher about their custom. In this case, a well-meaning teacher who lacked cultural knowledge about certain cultural experiences missed an opportunity to use the information in a meaningful way to enhance the learning for her Latino students. This teachable moment could have been used to discuss this custom, as well as reading and writing about many of the students' experiences of losing teeth. A math graph could have been constructed to graph the total number of teeth lost to "The Raton." In addition, the graph could have shown which students in class had lost the most and the least teeth. A trip to the library could have been taken to research other stories and customs about who takes the teeth that are placed under the pillows of many children around the world. These are just a few examples of how a teacher's knowledge of the cultural nuances of the Latino culture can be used in a meaningful way in the classroom (Anderson & Roit, 1998; Zainuddin et al., 2002).

INTERCULTURAL UNDERSTANDING

Understanding the linguistic and cultural diversity of Latino families

Many teachers mistakenly assume that all Latinos are "the same" in all elements of culture. In fact nothing could be further from the truth. Latino students and their families are not homogeneous but reflect diversity within the many facets of culture. Cultural differences influence the way students behave, communicate, and learn. It is learned and shared by the family. At an early age, children observe what is valued in their families and communities, and those home values may conflict with those of their school (Zainuddin et al., 2002).

Diversity in language

Language is used for communicating meaning. For many Latino families, Spanish may be the language spoken at home for all purposes. For other families, language may consist of a mixture of some English and Spanish for varying purposes. The important factor for educational purposes is the knowledge of how language is used by Latino families to communicate, taking into consideration some understandings of their discourse (Ibarra, 2004).

As a classroom teacher I learned much from my students and their families, especially new Spanish words. Most teachers believe all Spanish-speaking students and their families speak in the same manner because "Spanish is Spanish." The reality is that all speak Spanish but may use different words depending on their region of origin. Some parents and their children speak Spanish very fast, while others may speak with a different accent. It is useful for teachers to know where their students come from in order to understand their language better (García, 2002).

INTERCULTURAL UNDERSTANDING

Therefore, teachers, even those who speak Spanish, may be able to access this information during parental conferences or home visits.

In my case, I had a situation in which I learned a new Spanish vocabulary word by accident. My students were accustomed to having a short recess in the morning. However, due to strong rains during most of the day, my students and I were stuck indoors for almost an entire day. When the rains subsided in the afternoon, I asked the students if they would like to walk outside to the blacktop for some air and stretching. They, of course, said, "Yes!" I asked them to follow me outside to the blacktop. I requested that they not step in the mud because I did not want mud all over the new carpet in our classroom. I, however, used the word "soquete" for mud. This was the only word for mud my family used. The students said OK and off we went. To my amazement, the students walked directly into the puddles of mud, splashing all the way to the blacktop. I had specifically asked them not to do that. I stopped them and asked why they had deliberately disobeyed me and stepped in the "soquete"? With a puzzled look, one student finally raised her hand and asked, "Teacher, ¿Qué es soquete?" I looked incredulously at her and pointed to the mud all over her shoes. She looked at me and said, "We call that 'lodo' (mud)." No wonder the students didn't obey me; they didn't understand my Spanish word for mud.

In another instance, I understood the importance of sending home letters in Spanish for my students, even as a new teacher. At the time, the school did not provide a school translator for outgoing school correspondence. However, I had a skillful classroom assistant who was very knowledgeable about the Latino culture and their language discourse. She routinely translated the school's correspondence to parents from English to Spanish. On one occasion, I reviewed her translation and became very annoyed with the manner in which she translated it. It read more like a letter I would have written to my best friend during my teenage years: "Hi, Nora. How are you? When you receive this letter, I hope that you are doing well. As for me and my family, we are fine. Thanks! . . ." The translation did not state: "Dear Parents: The purpose of this letter is to inform you that we will . . ." The school's letter was very direct and to the point. I questioned my assistant's style by indicating that her translation was not a direct translation from the English version being sent out to the other parents. I politely asked her to redo the translation. She, however, very tactfully convinced me to reconsider and leave the letter as she had translated it because the communication style was "friendly." She helped me to see that the English style of communicating is too direct and appears harsh for many Latinos (Zainuddin et al., 2002). If the English communication could be visually depicted, a straight arrow pointing down would be drawn. She would certainly translate the letter as a direct translation from the English version; however, she felt it would not be received well by the parents. In fact, I could be perceived as a cold and distant teacher, which is the last thing I wanted. After all, the translations were aimed at better communicating with Latino parents and establishing a pleasant rapport between school and home. For all the occasions in which we wanted to provide information for parents, the letter started somewhat informally. Then it might proceed in a more technical fashion within the letter, especially for giving specific information. On that day, I learned something very valuable when it came to style or discourse of communicating with Latino parents. It's not what you say, but how you say it. The way you connect with a group is by understanding their language nuances and using this information to improve communications (García, 2002).

INTERCULTURAL UNDERSTANDING

How can the teacher use the information about language in the classroom? First of all, students learn their communication from their language and families and how it is used for communicating purposes. In my case, I discovered if the discourse pattern of my students could be visually illustrated, it would probably resemble a jagged edge—going from one subject to another. When a student was asked to write a story about a special holiday, the tendency was to write as they spoke. If what the student wrote resembled the "jagged edge" pattern, a teacher might encourage the student to stick more closely to the main point. If the teacher recognizes this "jagged" tendency in writing, it should be recognized as something of value that is learned at home. However, it is also very important for the teacher to explicitly teach the English writing style, which is very direct and "to the point." In other words, the teacher is acknowledging the native pattern but is teaching the style of writing, more direct and to the point in nature, that will be tested on standardized exams. A culturally responsive teacher may allow students to write in their natural manner with informal writings such as journals or learning logs; however, students should be taught to write in the direct mode for purposes of standardized testing. This approach validates the language patterns many Latino students bring to school, while also explicitly teaching the style of writing that will allow them to be successful when tested (García, 2002).

What are the educational implications for knowing the above information about language? Knowing nuances of language and communication can have a dramatic effect on how the teacher instructs in the classroom, the activities and strategies used in language arts, and how to communicate effectively with parents. In other words, if the teacher knows students are not afforded much time to discuss school activities or express themselves fully at home, then adequate time slots should be devoted during class to develop a repertoire of rich oral language experiences, which will later transfer to reading and writing exercises. For example, as a classroom teacher, I would devote some time on Monday mornings for students to talk about what they did on the weekend. I wasn't being "nosey," but I understood this was time well spent because it provided students with an opportunity to reflect on their activities and to express themselves orally in complete sentences. Due to various factors, in many of my students' homes, large amounts of times were usually not devoted for lengthy conversations with children. Therefore, it was important for me to use classroom time to help develop oral language skills. It also provided a platform for discussions, questions, sharing, and getting to know each other better (Hill & Flynn, 2006). This time was also used for practicing English speaking skills on subsequent days.

Diversity in cultural experiences

The levels of educational attainment of Latino parents impact their educational experiences, expectations for their children, their involvement and participation in their children's school activities and projects, and many other areas. At times, educators have had the misconception that Latino parents do not want to become involved in their children's education because they do not participate or volunteer at school. However, once again nothing could be further from the truth. Many Latino parents indicate they do not "participate" for varying reasons. First of all, one or both parents may work two jobs to keep the family afloat financially, and there is not much time to devote to school activities or volunteering opportunities. Other reasons include inconvenient times to volunteer, lack of transportation to school, inability to speak English, or not feeling welcomed when visiting schools

(Robles-Goodwin, 2004). Latino parents also have many different perceptions of the school's role, and the role of the parents. Many Latino parents who may not have had much formal education could feel they cannot help out in schools because they themselves do not have the educational skills for assisting in the classroom. Others feel like they are "involved parents" because they get their children up, feed and dress them, and transport them to school. They feel they have completed "their duty." Now the teachers should do "their part," which is to teach. Latino parents may not understand why teachers ask them to become involved. Many view this plea as a sign that the teacher is "lazy" or not "well prepared" (Moreno & Valencia, 2002). What is certain is that a misunderstanding may occur on both sides regarding what is truly meant by schools and teachers reaching out to the community and parents in an effort to work together. The question is how can both teachers and parents better understand each other's perspectives?

Bridging the information gap

Two experienced Spanish bilingual teachers are called to the principal's office to address complaints from a group of Spanish-speaking parents with children in the bilingual program. The parents are concerned about the quality of educational experiences (or lack of them) in the area of literacy and question the preparedness of the two teachers.

In another situation two bilingual kindergarten teachers are at a loss as to why the parents view them as mediocre teachers when they both work hard to provide a teaching approach and philosophy that is developmentally, culturally, and educationally appropriate for their Latino students. All activities are completed with much planning and knowledge of current educational best practices for enhancing the literacy skills of ELLs, particularly

INTERCULTURAL UNDERSTANDING

Latino students. Furthermore, both bilingual teachers are fluent in Spanish. One is a native speaker, and the other learned Spanish by taking courses in high school and college.

After discussing the situation further with the principal, it is discovered the parents feel the students are not receiving enough worksheets to practice letter formation. Both teachers know they have been utilizing a variety of hands-on activities to enhance many of the literacy skills needed at the kindergarten level. Many emergent skills such as recognizing individual names of the alphabet letters are taught through literature. For example, they have been used to introduce different types of literary genres to the students as they have read and discussed each book, written story charts, made class books, written language experience stories, made Venn diagrams of two or more books to discuss similarities and differences, and conducted many other hands-on activities. The parents are correct: the teachers do not use worksheets in their teaching. If you ask the teachers why, they will state that the worksheets are not age or educationally appropriate to use with these young students. They believe there are other suitable ways to meet the same objectives without resorting to using worksheets. During lessons, the students are asked to think about the story and the main character(s). Teachers supply crayons and paper and ask the students to draw a different ending to the story or to imagine that they are the main character and to think of what they might have done differently than the decision made by the main character in the book. Since the kindergarten students have varying writing skills and experiences, the students are instructed to illustrate the story. Afterwards, the students dictate their stories to the teacher. The teacher then writes their stories. The drawings from each student are put together to create a class book for the students to "read." These books are chosen and "read" over and over by the

INTERCULTURAL UNDERSTANDING

students because they had a part in putting it together, and it has relevance to their lives.

In this instance, the two teachers could have easily become angry with the parents' concerns. Why didn't the parents just address their concerns with them? Why did they feel the need to talk to the principal, who didn't even speak Spanish? Needless to say, it was an awkward situation. Both teachers thought long and hard about how they would handle this situation for them. After much deliberation, it was concluded that a "talk" with the parents to address their concerns would not be effective. It could even become counterproductive or even combative. After all, they both knew that they were well-trained and utilizing current best teaching practices when working with Latino students.

The two teachers decided to invite the parents to come to school one evening for an hour so they could experience a daily literacy lesson their children completed that day. When the parents arrived, the teachers separated the parents into two groups, one half going with Teacher A and the other half with Teacher B. The parents working with Teacher A experienced reading of a story, discussion of characters, plot, and problem resolution, and exploration of their favorite character. Their responses were written by Teacher A on a large tablet and later read out loud. The concluding activity included giving each parent a piece of Manila paper and crayons for illustrating a different story ending of their own.

The group working with Teacher B experienced reading of a story, discussion, and a worksheet in which each parent had to write the letter "l" over and over again on a lined worksheet. The story was about a "lobo" (wolf), so the worksheet had a picture of a wolf on the center top half of the worksheet. The lower part had lines for the student to write the letter "l" over and over again. The parents in both groups assumed the role of students. For the last part of the meeting, both groups of parents were brought together for a debriefing of their experiences as students. They were asked to recall their experiences and to state what they had learned. While the parents shared, the teachers wrote their responses on the tablet. The parents with Teacher A commented on all the activities they had done. They also recalled having to "think" very much. They had to think about the story, their favorite part, and another ending. They commented on how it was fun and exciting but very hard work. After all statements were written on the tablet, the parents realized the word "think" came up over and over again. One parent stated that she thought so much it made her head hurt. Another parent commented on the fact that it was hard work to think on a "high level" before actually drawing his picture. Although the parents only saw the finished "art project" when their children brought home their school work, they now realized there indeed had been some in-depth thought and higher-level thinking prior to the drawings.

 The parents with Teacher B began to share their experiences. To sum up their responses, most of them listened to a story, discussed it, and then finished the worksheet with the wolf picture. They talked about how they just wrote the letter "l" (for "lobo") over and over again. One mother stated she got bored writing the letter "l" again and again. When asked what she learned, she said, "Nothing. While I was writing all those letters, I kept thinking about other things. I thought about what I needed to do after I got home from this meeting, like going to the grocery store or washing a load of laundry, ..."

 All of a sudden, one seemingly reticent father stood up and said, "Now I get it! I was one of the parents who complained to the principal about your teaching. I realize now that I was judging your competence and your teaching strategies based on the lack of worksheets. All I ever saw coming home were pictures with dictations. My thoughts were, 'I'm sending my children to school so they can play and draw pictures all day.' Now I understand!" He also recognized, as well as other parents, they were reverting back to the way in which they had been taught when in kindergarten. Many of them had been educated in different parts of Latin America. Their educational system had been very traditional with the reliance of a multitude of worksheets. Their teachers usually had up to 35 students at one time, so worksheets were common and probably helped the teacher regain a little time for grouping or transition activities. So, through this literacy reenactment with hands-on activities experienced in the classroom on a daily basis, the parents soon realized how much their children were learning while they were in school. They also expressed appreciation to the teachers for their hard work and understanding. They vowed to assist their children in any way necessary to help them continue learning. Ladson-Billings (1995) and Delpit (1995) reported that when the curriculum was connected to their backgrounds, the students were able to understand complex ideas even beyond their reading levels. Conversely, a continuous disconnect between the children's background may cause them to become disengaged with literacy activities (Ferdman, 1990).

While this story has a happy ending, the teachers learned much from this experience. They learned that although they were doing many good things in the classroom, they needed to do a better job of communicating with the parents about their goals, expectations, and strategies. In other words, they needed to find methods of communicating class projects, themes, fieldtrips, and other newsworthy information to parents. They decided to have a weekly newsletter titled "Esta Semana" (This Week). In this

INTERCULTURAL UNDERSTANDING

newsletter, the teachers briefly recaptured all the major events and learning for the week such as stories, poems, activities, upcoming events, requests, reminders, and special student commendations. This one-page newsletter was sent home with the students every Friday afternoon. As the year progressed, the teachers allowed the students more input on what would be depicted in the newsletter. The teacher also allowed students with artistic abilities to illustrate some events or even create some type of "clip art." The bottom line of the newsletters always ended with positive statements such as: "¡La escuela esta semana fue maravillosa!" (School this week was marvelous!). The compilation of the newsletter afforded the teachers an opportunity to recapture not only the daily activities, but also the week's learning.

In addition, teachers recognized the need to provide closure at the end of each day to allow the students to reflect on their learning. Therefore, during the last 10-15 minutes of each day, the teachers would ask the students, "What did you learn today?" The students' responses were written on a large tablet. So when the students' parents asked, "What did you learn today?", the students were ready to answer the question.

On the other hand, teachers not utilizing a weekly newsletter or closure to the day's learning before dismissal time later learned from parents that their children would always state they did not learn anything in school that day—even if that was not true. The problem was that the students simply were not given opportunities at school to reflect on learning and then discuss in advance.

After a while, the parents became accustomed to receiving the weekly newsletters. If a teacher was ill or was out for one reason or another and could not get the weekly newsletter out on Friday, the parents would call the school to report their Weekly Newsletter was missing. It became a great communication vehicle for this school and the teachers. The parents became "connected" to the teachers and the learning that was taking place at school (Moreno & Valencia, 2002).

In yet another instance, a mother of twin boys expresses concern because her sons were placed in two separate kindergarten classrooms. One son comes home every day enthusiastically talking about new stories, poems, and songs learned during the day, while the other one states he learned nothing.

In this scenario, the mother of the twin sons has concerns. One of her sons was in a class in which the teacher utilized a weekly newsletter, and the other was in a class in which the teacher did not. The mother expressed she could definitely tell the difference between her sons' educational experiences. One son always came home telling about a new story, song or poem, while the other did not. He enjoyed going to school, while the other one did not. One son appeared to be learning and progressing, while the other son appeared to just be "filling in the time." As for the mother's perception of the two teachers, she believed one to be exceptional, and the other mediocre.

The teachers using the weekly newsletters became the favorites for parents. These teachers recognized the importance of communicating with parents in a systematic way. Word got out that these teachers were the best in every way. Why? Why this sudden turn around in perceptions and attitudes about the teachers? What made the difference? These teachers were considered exceptional in their districts. One held a masters degree and the other a doctorate, but both had been misunderstood by their Latino parents. The teachers had not understood the importance of communicating and connecting with the Latino parents in their community. The weekly newsletter gave them one outlet needed for consistent communications. Other outreaches utilized throughout the year were conferences with parent and occasional home visits. Parents can support schools only if they are kept abreast of the changes occurring in school practices and instruction. Parents who are poorly informed cannot participate fully in schools (King & Goodwin, 2002; Moreno & Valencia, 2002).

Tapping into strategies that work

Traditional ways of reaching out to Latino parents have not been traditionally culturally responsive. Schools today should aim for being creative in their outreach attempts to improve communications with Latino parents. Many times, it will take an "out of the box" plan to accomplish this mission (Moreno & Valencia, 2002). These endeavors can be accomplished through informal conversations with them, home visits, parent conferences, surveys or whatever other methods work for a particular school. One creative school recognized Latino parents were not able to attend school meetings and assemblies for parents in the evening, so the school began offering a session in Spanish at the party room of the apartment complex that most of their students lived. This outreach had never been attempted, but it appeared to be effective in reaching out to a large number of parents not able to come to the school.

Home visits

Another way to learn more about how families communicate with each other is to observe them. Many cultural facets can be viewed first hand by visiting the homes of families. For example during home visits, it is interesting to note interactions between adults and children—to observe the many verbal and nonverbal ways they communicate with each other. Many times, silence can symbolize respect, especially toward older relatives. Do children listen to or interact with adults? What is the role of the child? Do the adults expand on children's leads in conversations? Many children are not allowed to interrupt an adult's conversation, while other families encourage all to participate in conversations and storytelling.

Because of the changing times, attitudes, misunderstandings, lack of time, and many other reasons, home visits do not seem to be as common as they used to be. As a professor, I advocate for this practice but many of my pre-service teachers tend to fixate on the dangerous reasons why it should not be done today instead of focusing on the benefits. As a teacher, my principals recognized the value of connecting with Latino parents in a very unique way only accomplished through home visits, especially visiting families that were unable to come to school. The principals allowed teachers to visit and become familiar with the school's community since most teachers did not live in the same community. The benefits were invaluable for both me and my families. I was treated like royalty, and most importantly, my students felt the same because their teacher had visited their home. These visits, allowed me and the parents to get to know each other in an informal and comfortable setting. I was able to meet fathers I had not met due to their work schedules, see extended family members, meet pets, discover the interests of the family, see hobbies, see the home environment, and see the surrounding community. It also was a time to learn about the parents' perspectives, concerns, goals, and aspirations as they related to their children. In my interviews with hundreds of parents, I never interviewed a single parent that did not have high goals and educational aspirations for their children. They always wanted their children to "have more than they had—more education, more opportunities." The only barrier to meeting these goals was they didn't seem to have a plan or the facility for accessing resources. For example, they wanted their children to attend college; however, many of them did not have a financial plan to pay for it and were unable to relate to the college experience (Robles-Goodwin, 2004). Home visits are golden moments for caring teachers to intervene and provide guidance to parents in these areas. After my home visits, I had a greater understanding of my students' home environments and a better understanding of what was relevant or meaningful to them. The information learned was then translated to the school environment.

For instance, on one of my home visits, I arrived to find my student outside his apartment looking for bugs. He was fascinated by all types of bugs. One day, he arrived early at school with his hands behind him. He asked me to close my eyes and extend my hands out because he had a big surprise for me. Because students usually brought me apples, weeds (or wild flowers), and other things, I complied. To my disbelief, I felt something "buggy" crawling up my arm. I screamed and opened my eyes. My student looked at me and said, "Isn't he beautiful?" I realized he had given me something that was very precious to him. After breathing again, I incorporated a "bug" theme in my science center. He especially enjoyed the addition of silkworms in the spring.

Teachers conducting home visits tend to better understand the personal home situations that may impact the learning experience at school. The habit of a student falling asleep during class is now understood because it was observed that the student shared a room with two teenage brothers that may have work schedules that conflict with school bedtimes (Robles-Goodwin, 2006).

INTERCULTURAL UNDERSTANDING

During home visits to Latino homes, teachers from a successful school reported seeing many types of exotic birds or parrots as pets (Robles-Goodwin, Mohr, & Wilhelm, 2005; Wilhelm, Robles-Goodwin, & Mohr, 2005). With this knowledge, some teachers decided to incorporate a unit on birds into their integrated curriculum. During language arts, they read books on birds, wrote stories about birds; and in art, they made paper maché birds. All content areas addressed were taught by incorporating the bird theme. Student interest in this theme was high because it was one they could relate to. The teachers went a step farther in their responsive approach by inviting parents to bring their birds to school to share their "expert" knowledge on caring for these pets. This school recognized a successful way to connect to the Latino parents and to infuse the specific knowledge learned during home visits into their teaching. With this successful experience, the school had extended the "welcome mat" and the parents were now visiting on a frequent basis. In fact, another class invited several mothers to come and share the cultural tradition of making tamales during the winter holidays (Robles-Goodwin, et al., 2005; Wilhelm, et al., 2005).

Parent conferences

Parent conferences should be planned deliberately with very specific goals. Something that I found very helpful during parent conferences was to ask parents to relay any particular information that I needed to know about the student that would help me as the classroom teacher. This information could range from learning challenges or disabilities, illnesses, or any family traditions or childrearing practices, customs, etc. For example, many Latino parents instruct their children to look down when they are being disciplined. Although this practice varies from family to family, this behavior is seen as a sign of respect toward the authority figure in the family. It seems that more recent arrivals to this country are more apt to adhere to this tradition of respect to elders than first or second generation Latino students. This custom, however, has the opposite effect in U.S. schools, where many American teachers see the lowering of the eyes as a sign of disrespect toward them (Hildebrand, Phenice, Gray, & Hines, 2000).

During parent conferences or informal occasions with the teacher, Latino parents always seem to ask teachers, "¿Cómo se comporta mi hijo?" (How does my child behave at school?) A child's behavior is very important to many Latino parents. They always admonish their children to behave well at school. For many Latino parents, a sign of an educated person is one that behaves appropriately, especially at school. Some Latino students know they may be punished twice for misbehaving—once at school and again at home (Hildebrand et al., 2000). As a teacher, I worked with another teacher who stated how much trouble a certain student was giving her in terms of behavior. She stated how she had tried different types of approaches, but none of them seemed to make a difference. She identified the student. I was surprised to learn of his behavior, especially since I knew the student and the family very well. This family was hard-working in which the father held down two jobs to support the family. I asked the teacher if I could talk to this student. She gladly accepted my offer since none of her strategies had worked. When I walked into the classroom and approached this student, I expressed how disappointed I was to hear of his behavior. I also commented on how sad his father would feel when notified of his behavior, especially since he worked so hard to make sure his children attended school. He quickly looked up with much remorse for his conduct and asked me not to contact his father. The news of his behavior would indeed make his father very sad, and he did not want to disappoint him. He promised to "change his ways" immediately. I informed the teacher about the student's effort to follow the rules in a respectful manner. A couple of days later, the teacher asked me what I had done because the student's behavior had changed completely. The solution wasn't magical. What the teacher didn't realize is that I understood something about how important respect is in a Latino family, especially when it comes to the parents. The good or bad behavior of students in schools usually reflects upon their parents. La Roche and Shriberg (2004) define "respeto" (respect) as a cultural value that centers on obedience toward parents and elders. Many Latino children are taught to comply with authority figures. Specific knowledge of the culture helped with the manner in which the student was "disciplined" (Hildebrand et al. 2000; Lynch et al., 2004).

Parent conferences are also very useful for helping Latino parents understand the programs and services their children may be receiving at school. For example, many Latino parents I interviewed did not know if their children were receiving bilingual or English as a Second Language (ESL) services at school, even though parental permission is required in order for students to be placed in these programs (Robles-Goodwin, 2004). Furthermore, many Latino parents with limited English skills and children, who also had similar language levels, rejected bilingual/ESL services for them. When questioned about their decisions, many reported they did not want their children in remedial classrooms. It was apparent that these parents were misinformed about the goals and purposes of placing qualified students in the bilingual program. Schools need to have some type of an informational session to inform Latino parents about the educational services available to their children. These services, if done well, can certainly accelerate English proficiency and learning. However, if parents reject the services, many Latino students are placed in English-only classrooms without any special language assistance to learn English. While some students survive without the help, others simply fall behind academically each year. Through parent conferences, misconceptions about the bilingual program can be discussed and clarified.

Recommendations for reaching goals

Educators generally agree that effective teaching requires mastery of content knowledge, including pedagogical skills. However, too many teachers are inadequately prepared to teach ethnically diverse students. Many teacher education programs still debate the best way of incorporating multicultural education in their courses, despite the increasing percentage of minority students performing poorly that will be encountered when pre-service teachers enter the classroom (Garcia, 2002; Hildebrand et al., 2000; Nieto, 2004). Explicit knowledge about the cultural diversity of many groups, including in-group differences, is imperative to meeting the needs of ethnically and culturally diverse students. Much of the current research on working with Latinos is not comprehensive in addressing the variables that make them a diverse group (Garcia, 2002; Hildebrand et al., 2000; Nieto, 2004). For example, the culture of recent arrivals to the U.S. varies greatly as compared to first or second generation Latinos. The information available about the Latinos has the tendency of portraying all Latinos as recent immigrants. Latinos vary culturally when considering how long they have been in the U.S., including the types of challenges they will experience in schools. In fact, much more research needs to be conducted on biracial families with Latino heritage in terms of cultural identities and the impact on teaching these students (Moreno et al., 2002). There is no "one approach fits all" when working with Latino students and their families. It has been the author's experience in interviewing Latino parents in Spanish that there is not enough research being conducted that actually involves talking to Spanish-speaking parents, especially those who do not speak any English, in an effort to get their feelings, impressions, and perceptions regarding educational issues (Robles-Goodwin, 2004; Robles-Goodwin, 2006). The following recommendations are offered in an effort to assist teachers in gaining a better understanding of the cultural variability of Latino students.

- Incorporate into teacher education programs curricula that address the diversity of Latino students and their families such as folklore, celebrations, traditions, and beliefs. The impact of intra-group diversity on teaching and learning should be emphasized when preparing future teachers for diverse classrooms.
- Demonstrate commitment to meaningful and culturally responsive home-school collaborations by creating a mission statement and setting yearly goals (King & Goodwin, 2002). This task should be done collectively as a school to include a variety of personnel such office staff, teachers, campus administrators, and parent representatives, especially for "buy-in" purposes.
- Strong parental involvement in a child's education is essential to the success of the child and school. Schools with large Latino numbers should develop creative and comprehensive ways to ensure that parents are connected to the school's culture, purpose, and organization.

INTERCULTURAL UNDERSTANDING

- Plan a series of parent-focus groups, parent-teacher seminars or parent-teacher team-building activities based on survey/interview findings.
- Improve communications with Latino parents by asking for their input in creative ways and keeping them informed. These endeavors can be accomplished through informal conversations with them, classroom newsletters, home visits, parent conferences, surveys or whatever other methods work in a particular community.
- Create a cultural resource binder for keeping valuable information such as personnel resources, translators, community organizations, and free health clinics. This binder can become a resource to teachers, families, and visitors.
- Designate a space or room for parents. This resource space for families should be inviting. It should be a place for accessing resources, reading, and meeting with other parents or just getting a cup of coffee. A formalized space sends a strong welcoming message to families.
- Utilize Latino teachers as resources for the school to accomplish outreach initiatives. However, it should <u>not</u> be assumed that a Latino teacher will be familiar with all the cultural variability encountered among Latino families.
- Recognize that Latinos are culturally and linguistically diverse, and their length of time in the U.S. impacts their acculturation into American schools. For example, not all Latinos are recent arrivals to this country. Many are now first or second generation Latinos.
- Incorporate elements and themes of the Latino culture into the school curriculum and integrate it throughout all subject areas. For example, a teacher can use examples students

can relate to when writing a story for language arts or when the teacher gives a story problem for solving a math problem.

Conclusion

A culturally responsive teaching approach attempts to increase the academic achievement of students by making learning more relevant and meaningful to their experiences and frames of references. Neuman (1999) posits that culturally responsive instruction focuses on recognizing and valuing children's home cultures, promoting collaboration, holding high standards for all children, and appreciating the continuity between children's home life and their school literacy experiences. Traditionally, the goals and structure of public schools in the U.S. has not reflected values conducive to success of Latino students. Demographics for Latinos in U.S. schools require innovative approaches and outreaches for better understanding and working with Latino families in today's schools.

This article has suggested ways teachers and schools can reach out to Latino families in a variety of ways in order to understand more about their diverse culture. A one-size-fits-all approach to working with Latino families should not be used. An individualized framework accommodating for cultural variability of Latinos should be recognized and used when considering curricular decisions. The knowledge gained should be used to provide a more culturally responsive curriculum and approach that recognizes meaningful and reciprocal connections between school and home settings.

Through thoughtful and deliberate school efforts to better understand the diversity of Latino families in U.S. schools, educators can begin to plan for specific strategies to encourage mutual collaboration between school and home. This type of initiative can greatly enhance the educational achievement of Latino students as well as provide a nurturing environment for teaching and learning.

References

Anderson, V., & Roit, M. (1998). Reading as a gateway to language proficiency for language-minority students in the elementary grades. In R. M. Gersten & R. T. Jiménez (Eds.), *Promoting learning for culturally and linguistically diverse students* (pp. 42-54). Albany, NY: Wadsworth Publishing Company.

Au, K. H. (1994). Cultural congruence in instruction. In E. R. Hollins, J. E. King, & W. C. Hayman (Eds.), *Teaching diverse populations: Formulating a knowledge base* (pp. 5-23). Albany, NY: State University of New York Press.

August, D. (2006). Demographic overview. In D. August & T. Shanahan, (Eds.), *Developing literacy in second-language learners: Report of the National Literacy Panel* (pp. 43-49). Mahwah, NJ: Lawrence Erlbaum Associates, Publishers.

Capps, R., Fix, M. E., & Reardon-Anderson, J. (2003). Children of immigrants show slight reductions in poverty, hardships. *Snapshots of America's families III: A view of the nation and 13 states from the national survey of American families.* Washington, DC: Urban Institute.

Chafel, J. A. (1997). Societal images of poverty: Child and adult beliefs. *Youth & Society, 28*(4), 432-464.

Chall, J. S., Jacobs, V. A., & Baldwin, E. E. (1990). *The reading crisis: Why poor children fall behind.* Cambridge, MA: Harvard University Press.

Delpit, L. (1995). *Other people's children: Cultural conflict in the classroom.* New York: New Press.

Ferdman B. (1990). Literacy and cultural identity. *Harvard Education Review, 60,* 179-204.

Gay, Geneva (2000). *Culturally responsive teaching: Theory, research, and practice.* New York: Teachers College Press.

García, E. (2002). *Student cultural diversity: Understanding and meeting the challenge.* New York: Houghton Mifflin Company.

Green, E. J. (1997). Guidelines for serving linguistically and culturally diverse young children. *Early Childhood Journal, 24*(3), 147-154.

Hildebrand, V., Phenice, L. A., Gray, M. M., & Hines, R. P. (2000). *Knowing and serving diverse families.* Upper Saddle River, NJ: Prentice-Hall.

Hill, J. D., & Flynn, K. M. (2006). *Classroom instruction that works with English language learners.* Alexandria, VA: Association for Supervision and Curriculum Development.

Hollins, E. R (1996). *Culture in school learning: Revealing the deep meaning.* Mahwah, NJ: Lawrence Erlbaum.

Ibarra, R. A. (2004). Academic success and the Latino family. In R. E. Ybarra & N. López (Eds.), *Creating alternative discourses in the education of Latinos and Latinas* (pp. 113-132). New York: Peter Lang Publishing.

Jalango, M. R. (1996). On behalf of children: Pervasive myths about poverty and young children. *Early Childhood Education Journal, 24*(1), 1-3.

Jiménez, R. T. (2002). Fostering the literacy development of Latino students. *Focus on Exceptional Children, 34*(6), 1-10.

Kagan, S. L., & García, E. E. (1991). Educating culturally and linguistically diverse preschoolers: Moving the agenda. *Early Childhood Research Quarterly,* 6, 427-43.

King, S. H., & Goodwin, A. L. (2002). *Culturally responsive parental involvement: Concrete understandings and basic strategies.* Washington, DC: American Association of Colleges for Teacher Education.

Klein, M. D., & Chen, D. (2001). *Working with children from culturally diverse backgrounds*. Albany, NY: Delmar, Thomson Learning.

Ladson-Billings, G. (1995). Toward a theory of culturally relevant pedagogy. *American Educational Research Journal, 32*(3), 465-491.

LaRoche, M. J., & Shriberg, D. (2004). High stakes exams and Latino students: Toward a culturally sensitive education for Latino children in the United States. *Journal of Educational and Psychological Consultation, 15*(2), 205-223.

Lynch, E. W., & Hanson, M. J. (2004). *Developing cross-cultural competence: A guide for working with children and families*. Baltimore, MD: Paul H. Brooks Publishing Company.

McLoyd, V. C. (1995). Poverty, parenting, and policy: Meeting the support needs of poor parents. In H. E. Fitzgerald & B. M. Lester (Eds.), (pp. 269-303), *Children of poverty: Research, health, and policy issues*. New York: Garland Publishing, Inc.

Moreno, R. P., & Valencia R. R. (2002). Chicano families and schools: Myths, knowledge, and future directions for understanding. In R. R. Valencia (Ed.), *Chicano school failure and success: Past, present, and future*. New York: Routledge Falmer.

Nieto, S. (2004). *Affirming diversity: The sociopolitical context of multicultural education*. Boston: Pearson Education, Inc.

Neuman, S. B., & Roskos, K. (1994). Bridging home and school with a culturally responsive approach. *Childhood Education, 70*, 210-214.

Okagaki, L., & Diamond, K. E. (2000). Responding to cultural and linguistic differences in the beliefs and practices of families with young children. *Young Children, 55*(3), 74-80.

Prince, C., & Lawrence, L. (1993). School readiness and language minority students: Implications of the first national education goal. *FOCUS/Occasional Papers in Bilingual Education, 7*. Washington, DC: National Clearinghouse for Bilingual Education.

Robles-Goodwin, P. J. (2004, December). *Leave no parent behind. . .: An investigation into the educational perceptions of Latino parents with young children in urban, suburban, and rural school settings.* Paper presented at the meeting of the Hawaii International Conference on Education, Honolulu, Hawaii.

Robles-Goodwin, P. J., Mohr, K. A. J., & Wilhelm, R. W. (2005). An investigation into the effective teaching practices and perceptions of Latino parents regarding their educational experiences. Paper presented at the meeting of the *American Educational Research Association (AERA)*, Montreal, Canada.

Robles-Goodwin (2006). Understanding English language learners: Challenges and promises. In P. Dam & M. T. Cowart (Eds.), *Cultural and linguistic issues for English language learners* (pp. 56-82). Denton, TX: Federation of North Texas Area Universities.

U.S. Census Bureau. (2001). *School enrollment in the United States—Social and economic characteristics of students.* Washington, DC: U.S. Department of Commerce.

Valencia, R. R. (2002). The explosive growth of the Chicano/Latino population: educational implications. In Richard R. Valencia, (Ed.), *Chicano school failure and success: Past, present, and future.* New York: Routledge Falmer.

Wilhelm, R. W., Robles-Goodwin, P. J., & Mohr, K. A. (2005). Engaging Latino learners: A re-examination of English-only immersion. Paper presented at the meeting of the *American Educational Research Association (AERA),* Montreal, Canada.

Zainuddin, H., Yahya, N., Morales-Jones, C.A., & Ariza, E.N. (2002). *Fundamentals of teaching English to speakers of other languages in K-12 Mainstream Classrooms.* Dubuque, IA: Kendall/Hunt Publishing Company.

Supporting Positive Home-School Connections with Ethnic Minority Parents

Dora L. Salazar
Texas Tech University

Mary F. B. Garza
Midwestern State University

Many educators believe that strengthening family involvement in schools is one of the most important ways to improve student school success (Aronzon, 1996; Ballen & Moles, 1994; Lee & Bowen, 2006). Often, teachers view parental non-involvement as a lack of interest in their children's achievement. Conversely, some ethnic minority parents do not feel comfortable attending school events. Therefore, understanding the ways schools either support and sustain or limit and suspend home-school connections can help more children achieve. This article begins by describing connection between family involvement and student achievement. We examine possible perceptual differences present in existing home-school participation structures, and conclude with suggestions to enhance home-school interactions for Mexican American parents.

Family-school connections

Research shows that the strongest association between parental involvement and student achievement is enjoyed by European American middle-class parents and their children;

however, it also reports that ethnic minority parental involvement has a positive effect on the academic achievement of their children (Jeynes, 2003; Lee & Bowen, 2006). Some studies examine the degree and type of participation experienced by ethnic minority parents (Delgado-Gaitán, 1991). This body of work describes the extent to which families feel welcomed in school, and reveals differences in home-school perception (Delgado-Gaitán, 1991; Vandegrift & Greene, 1992; Whitehead, 1993). Additionally, Epstein (1995) points out that most schools use six types of parental involvement: parenting, communicating, volunteering, learning at home, decision making, and collaborating with the community. Each type, generic in nature, has a purpose. All have a different impact on home-school linkages. All place some degree of restriction on the opportunities for diverse parents to participate in school events.

Perceptual differences in participation structures

A problem emerges when schools, perhaps inadvertently, do not take into account differences among the economic, linguistic, and cultural values, skills, and experiences of the children and parents involved (Gay, 2000; Nieto, 2005; Sheets, 2005). For example, past research shows that many communication strategies directed at ethnic minority and low-income families tend to (a) alert parents of misbehavior and low academic achievement, or (b) focus on negative school perceptions of the home, such as poor parenting skills, degrees of English proficiency, or (c) include directives related to the perceived limitations in the experiences, skills, and knowledge of parents and children (Villegas, 1991). Consequently, repeated written and oral messages from schools to Mexican American parents tell them to speak in English to their children or to help them with homework. Both of these messages can be perceived as insensitive to parenting skills, values and needs of this ethnic minority group. Parents are generally proud of their children's developing bilingualism. Most believe that their home language benefits their children. They view Spanish as a cultural tool necessary to the maintenance of strong cultural familial connections. Thus, being asked to stop speaking their heritage language by teachers whom they respect can generate discomfort and conflict. Their frustration in helping with homework and a cultural belief that they should not interfere with the ways school teach can generate frustration and feelings of inadequacy. Parents who do not help their children with homework may cause some teachers to view families as lazy, apathetic, or uncaring about their child's learning. Contrasting sentiments on both parts serve to distance rather than encourage positive child-school-parent relationships.

Thus, schools and teachers can unwittingly disenfranchise parents by providing letters, memos, newsletters, or other traditional contact methods and requirements, such as uninvited home visits, mandatory parent-teacher conferences, imposed parental workshops, use of material enticements, or weekly discipline or work folders requiring parental signatures. These forms of communication on the surface may seem appropriate, but could actually cause undue stress in the home. Some parents may not be able to take a day off from work to attend parent-teacher conferences if they are held only during regular work hours. Families may feel embarrassed of their economic status and their less than perfect living conditions. Workshops in English for Spanish-speaking parents may seem irrelevant regardless of the content, or weekly discipline folders requiring a parent's signature may be signed without parents understanding the purpose of this practice. Some districts use material incentives to entice parents and promote involvement. These may include invitations to a district's clothes closet or handing out vouchers for the local grocery stores. While most parents will not inform the school of their discomfort, some may not want to be viewed as charity cases, or they may choose to keep private their use of second-hand clothing for their child.

The home-school connection

Schools which understand the cultural values and needs of diverse parents can translate this knowledge base to culturally responsive home-school activities (Gay, 2000). Some culturally inclusive interventions that successfully bridge home and school can include (a) providing qualified interpreters or community-selected liaisons for scheduled home visits and parent-teacher conferences, (b) validating parent volunteers with access and space within the entire campus, (c) translating written messages, and (d) inviting families to school functions such as awards assemblies, math competitions, plays, musicals, debates, spelling bees, chess games, and sport activities. However, assumptions cannot be made that ethnic minority parents who regularly attend school functions are automatically involved in leadership roles or in decision-making positions. Sometimes, involved parents will feel embarrassed if their low level of education limits their participation, especially if schools are reluctant to involve them in meaningful roles and perceive them more as a problem rather than a helper (Sheets, 2005).

In addition, family involvement in the school setting can effectively address specific academic and social needs of ethnic minority parents. Standardized home-school participation policies and practices can be adapted or changed. Schools' participatory structures can take into consideration the parents' needs for alternative meeting times and places. The nature of their home routines, literacy practices, and cultural values can be incorporated into home-school participation designs. This suggests that schools, willing to serve parental needs, must be ready to accommodate in ways that (a) encourage higher levels of acceptance of cultural differences, (b) build a knowledge base to promote cultural and linguistic understandings, (c) develop respectful levels of trust, and (d) promote strategies to strengthen and sustain equitable relationships.

Involvement of Mexican American families

While various models of parental involvement have been proposed, some do not examine and scrutinize how diverse cultural and linguistic variations dictate the extent to which parents can participate in school life. To improve the quality and quantity of participation of Mexican American parents, we propose attention should be given to the following:

Culturally safe atmosphere

- Establish a positive and friendly tone in all interactions through informal conversation, and when possible, provide light refreshments.

- Provide opportunities for teachers and parents to meet informally prior to scheduling formal meetings or required conferences. These steps could enhance teacher-parent communications and minimize feelings of discomfort and alienation.

INTERCULTURAL UNDERSTANDING

• Become aware of differences between the requirements of the U. S. public system and school expectations in their heritage country.

Example: In the Mexican American culture it is polite to inquire about the family members or to ask if you can be of assistance prior to beginning the actual task at hand. You might offer the parents a cup of coffee, give them time to become comfortable with their surroundings, and inquire about their family before giving information regarding their child's progress.

Cultural parameters

• Seek understanding of parents' prior home-school experiences and the extent of their involvement in previous school settings, especially if this was carried out in another cultural or national setting. This knowledge base can provide greater awareness for school personnel in this country.

• Include parent-teacher discussions regarding areas where cultural differences might occur.

• Offer professional development for teachers to enhance their awareness of how views held by school may potentially conflict with the values modeled in the child's home.

• Identify and process possible cultural barriers.

Example: Differences between appropriate personal space and acceptable speaking tone and volume can affect communication. Speaking distance varies among cultures. Speech considered loud in some cultures may be perceived as normal in others. In the Mexican

INTERCULTURAL UNDERSTANDING

American culture, the teacher is viewed as an authority figure; thus, summoning parents for a conference can be interpreted as scolding in nature. Therefore, it is important for teachers to use a professional, soft, and pleasant voice to diffuse the possibly negative connotation of the meeting.

<u>Shared roles</u>

- Provide an open and welcoming place where discussions include how parents see their roles as parents and how they view the role of the teacher as part of their child's life at school.

- Include conversations that provide opportunities for the parents to state their expectations for schooling as it pertains to their children within the U.S. public school system, as they understand it.

- Be aware that some parents may choose to discuss the reasons for their leaving a home country and the conditions leading to this decision.

<u>Cultural brokers</u>

- Identify individuals who can serve the cultural community as advocates for families. These advocates generally understand how their neighborhoods work, and may serve as valuable liaisons between the school and the community.

- Assist the parents in selecting leaders from within their own communities. Individuals chosen should be those preferred by parents themselves as they are usually active within their cultural circles of influence and are generally seen as leaders.

Conclusions

Creating a supportive learning environment requires an understanding of cultural, social, and linguistic factors that reach beyond the classroom into the homes of children. With respect to home-school relationships, teachers should be cognizant of the ways in which meaningful communication may be affected by language differences and cultural values. Awareness of parents' perceptions of schooling and the expectations they have for their children can enhance, build, and develop home-school bonds. Knowledge of home routines and belief systems is critical to promote effective parent involvement. Schools can be a welcoming place for all parents. Since data show persistent underachievement for children identified as English language learners, it is especially critical that home-school-community connections for this group become a priority.

References

Aronson, J. Z. (1996, April). How schools can recruit hard-to-reach parents. *Educational Leadership, 53*(7), 58-60.

Ballen, J., & Moles, O. (1994, September). *Strong families, strong schools: Building community partnerships for learning.* Washington, DC: U.S. Department of Education. Retrieved from: http://eric-web.tc.columbia.edu/families/strong/

Delgado-Gaitán, C. (1991). Involving parents in the school: A process for empowerment. *American Journal of Education, 100* (1), 20-46.

Epstein, J. L. (1995). School/family/community partnerships: Caring for the children we share. *Phi Delta Kappan, 76*(9), 705-707.

Gay, G. (2000). *Culturally responsive teaching: Theory, research and practice.* New York: Teachers College Press.

Jeynes, W. H. (2003). A meta-analysis: The effects of parental involvement on minority children's academic achievement. *Education and Urban Society, 35*(2), 202-218.

Lee, J. S., & Bowen, N. K. (2006). Parental involvement, cultural capital, and the achievement gap among elementary school children. *American Educational Research Journal, 43*(2), 193-218.

Nieto, S. (2005). *Affirming diversity: The sociopolitical context of multicultural education* (2nd ed.). New York: Longman.

Sheets, R. H. (2005). *Diversity pedagogy: Examining the role of culture in the teaching-learning process.* Boston: Allyn & Bacon.

Vandegrift, J.A., & Greene, A.L. (1992). Rethinking parent involvement. *Educational Leadership, 50* (1), 57-59.

Villegas, A. (1991). *Culturally responsive pedagogy for the 1990s and beyond.* Princeton, NJ: Educational Testing Service.

Whitehead, B.J. (1993). *An educational guide for parents of language minority students at Johnson Park School.* Unpublished master's thesis, California State University, Chico.

Glossary of Key Terms and Concepts in Intercultural Understanding

Rudy Rodríguez
University of North Texas

Melinda Cowart
Texas Woman's University

Phap Dam
Texas Woman's University

This list of lexical items is presented as a collection of the more common terms and concepts relevant to intercultural understanding. The glossary is drawn from several principal sources shown in the reference section. No attempt is made to present an all-inclusive or exhaustive compilation of major terms and concepts in the field.

Academic Standards: Setting standards that all students must meet, regardless of language proficiency level or ability (Ovando et al., 2003).

Acculturation: This refers to the process of transfer or borrowing of cultural elements between different cultures, resulting in new and blended patterns of behavior (Banks, 1986). According to Cortés (1993), acculturation should be the primary goal of the schools. Schools have the responsibility to help students acculturate, because additive acculturation contributes to individual "empowerment and expanded life choices." According to Brown (1994), the first stage of acculturation "is the period of excitement and euphoria over the newness of the surroundings. The second stage—culture shock—emerges as individuals feel the intrusion of more cultural differences into their own images of self and security. In this stage individuals rely on and seek out the support of their fellow countrymen in the second culture, taking solace in complaining about local customs and conditions, seeking escape from their predicament. The third stage is one of gradual, and at first tentative and vacillating, recovery. But general progress is made, slowly but surely, as individuals begin to accept the differences in thinking and feeling that surround them, slowly becoming more empathic with other persons in the second culture. The fourth stage represents near or full recovery, either assimilation or adaptation, acceptance of the new culture and self-confidence in the 'new' person that has developed in this culture" (p.171).

Additive Bilingual Programs: Additive bilingual programs are bilingual/dual language programs whose goal is bilingualism and bi-literacy for all students that participate. These programs are characterized by a late exit from either a dual language or maintenance bilingual education program, with instruction occurring in both English and Spanish (or another native language, L1).

Acquisition-Learning Hypothesis: Based on this hypothesis, there are two separate processes for the development of ability in second language: (1) via language acquisition which is similar to the way children develop their L1 competence and, (2) via language learning which is an explicit presentation of rules and grammar with the emphasis on error correction (Krashen, 1982).

Affective Domain: The emotional aspects of an individual's inner life, including attitudes, feelings, dispositions. For English language learners these affective or emotional factors include their attitudes and feelings towards language learning and the target language and culture.

INTERCULTURAL UNDERSTANDING

Affective Filter: According to Krashen (1982), the following affective variables are related to success in second language acquisition:
Anxiety -- low anxiety, e.g., the more comfortable the students are, the better the acquisition.
Motivation -- higher intrinsic motivation leads to more successful second language acquisition.
Self-confidence -- the acquirer with more self-esteem and self-confidence tends to do better in second language acquisition.

Assimilation: This refers to the acceptance by individuals from different ethnic heritages of the beliefs, values, and lifestyles of a national culture (Banks, 1986). In extreme assimilation, the individuals sever their identification with their ancestral group. Assimilation education is subtractive, according to Cortés (1993), because it encourages students to leave behind their ethnic and cultural beliefs and practices.

Audiolingual Approach: In this approach to second language development, there is dependence on mimicry and memorization of set phrases. This approach is based on the premise that language learning is habit formation. Skills are sequenced into listening, speaking, reading, and writing. Structural patterns are taught using repetitive drills. This method is based on theories from structural linguistics and behavioral psychology.

Basic Interpersonal Communication Skills (BICS): BICS, as distinguished from CALP, refers to language proficiency that is usually context embedded and is used for interpersonal communication. It can generally be acquired in a relatively short period of time.

Biculturalism: The ability to actively participate in a culture other than one's own.

INTERCULTURAL UNDERSTANDING

Bilingual Education Act: Formerly Title VII of the Elementary and Secondary Education Act (ESEA) signed by President Lyndon B. Johnson on January 2, 1968. Through this Act, the federal government made its first attempt to addressing the educational needs of language-minority students (Ovando et al., 2003).

Bilingual Education: A bilingual education program, generally defined, is one which is organized with the following three goals in mind:
1) The continued development of the student's primary language (L1);
2) Acquisition of the second language (L2), which for language minority students is English; and
3) Instruction in the content areas utilizing both L1 and L2.

Bilingual education is also defined as the use of both source or native language and target or second language as media of instruction in all or part of the curriculum. Study of the history and culture associated with a student's mother tongue is considered an integral part of bilingual education.

Bilingual Schooling: This refers to the particular organizational scheme of instruction which is used to mediate curricula in the home language and in another language.

Biliteracy: At its most basic level, biliteracy refers to a person's ability to read and write in two languages. The concept, however, has taken on a sociopolitical dimension, especially as reflected in the work of Brazilian educator Paulo Freire, who links literacy with issues of social justice and empowerment.

Code-Switching: This refers to a change by a speaker (or writer) from one language to another. Code-switching can take place in a conversation when one speaker uses one language and the other speaker answers in a different language. Example: *Fuimos* al dance; I'm going to Lupe's *a las cuatro* (Richards, J.C., Platt, J., & Platt, H., 1992).

Cognitive Academic Language Learning (CALLA): CALLA is designed for language minority students who are being prepared to participate in mainstream content area instruction. CALLA provides transitional instruction for upper elementary and secondary students at intermediate and advanced ESL levels. This approach furthers academic language development in English through content area instruction in science, mathematics, and social studies (Chamot & O' Malley, 1987).

Cognitive-Academic Language Proficiency (CALP): CALP, as distinguished from BICS, is a dimension of language proficiency that is strongly related to literacy skills and is the category of language that is necessary for success in the content area classroom. CALP is generally highly decontextualized.

Comprehensible Input: According to a second language acquisition theory, we acquire language by obtaining comprehensible input—by understanding messages, by listening, looking, understanding and internalizing the words, phrases, concepts. Messages in second language are made comprehensible though the use of pictures, objects, actions, interaction, and context (Krashen, 1985).

Cognitive Approach: In this approach, communication or communicative competence (i.e., being able to understand and be understood) is emphasized. Language acquisition is seen as the rule, not habit formation; deductive explanation of grammar is preferred; pronunciation is de-emphasized. This approach evolved from Noam Chomsky's theories about how language is learned (Ovando, Collier, & Combs, 2003).

Concurrent Approach: The teacher alternates the use of English and the non-English language based on pedagogical and sociolinguistic considerations. The teacher alternates between languages to reinforce concepts, lexical terms, and cultural awareness. A language switch can occur in response to student-initiated cues (Jacobson, 1981).

Culturally Responsive Teaching: "Using the cultural knowledge, prior experiences, frames of reference, and performance styles of ethnically diverse students to make learning encounters more relevant to and effective for them" (Gay, 2000, p. 29).

Culture: This refers to the unique lifestyle and being of a particular group of people.
It consists of the behavior patterns, symbols, institutions, values, and other human-made components of a society (Banks, 1986). Nieto (2008) defines culture as the values, traditions, worldview, and sociopolitical relationships created, shared, and transformed by a group of people bound together by a common history, geographic location, language, social class, religion, or other shared identity.

Cultural Relativism: This principle refers to the ability to view and value another culture as though one were a member of the culture. As Gollnick and Chinn (2006) stated, "In essence, it is an attempt to view the world through the other individual's cultural lens" (p. 20).

Developmental Bilingual Education (also Maintenance Bilingual Education): Refers to bilingual/dual language classes of English language learners only. Time schedules vary, but by the third grade generally 50% of the instruction is in English and 50% is in the home language of the students. Students are allowed to continue learning the native or first language in a maintenance bilingual education program even after they have met the exit criteria for ELLs established by the state.

Discrimination: The unfair treatment of individuals or groups based upon categories such as ethnicity, race, religion, age, sexual orientation, social class, language, or exceptionality (Banks, 2007). It is an act that, according to Allport (1954), "comes about only when we deny to individuals or groups of people equality of treatment which they wish" (as cited in Pang, 2005, p. G-2).

Dual Language (One-Way): Refers to a bilingual/dual language class of ELLs. Content is taught initially in the native language with organized instruction in English as a second language.

Dual Language (Two-Way): Refers to bilingual/dual language classes of a cohort based of students whose home language is English and students whose home language is a language other than English. These classes are conducted in both English and the second language. The goal of this program is that all students in the cohort will be bilingual and biliterate in both languages of instruction. According to Freeman, Freeman, & Mercuri (2005), characteristics of a two-way dual language bilingual program include the following:
- Students include native English speakers and native speakers of another language.
- Students are integrated during most content instruction.
- Instruction is provided in two languages.
- Students become proficient in two languages.
- Student achievement in English for all students is equal to or exceeds that of students learning in English only.

Educational Linguistics: Educational linguistics is a branch of applied linguistics that deals with the relationship between language and education. (Richards, Platt, & Platt, 1992). An important course in educational linguistics would be one in language and linguistics for teachers, as proposed by Fillmore and Snow (2000). In that course, "Each area of linguistic study would be introduced by educational situations in which language is an issue. For example, the study of phonology could begin with an examination of interference problems that English language learners might have with the English sound system" (p. 32).

INTERCULTURAL UNDERSTANDING

Emic: A viewpoint from the stance of being a member of particular group. This would be an in-group perspective.

Enculturation: The process by which one acquires the essential characteristics of a particular culture and becomes proficient in its language as well as its ways of behaving and knowing.

Error Analysis: As a study and analysis of errors made by second language learners, error analysis can help educators identify strategies which learners use in language learning; explain the causes of learner errors; and obtain information on common difficulties in language learning, as an aid to teaching or in the preparation of instructional materials (Richards, Platt, & Platt, 1992).

Etic: A viewpoint as one who is not a member of a particular cultural group. This would be an outsider's perspective.

English Language Learners (formerly known as Limited English Proficient Students): English language learners (ELLs) are students whose first language is other than English and who are in the process of learning English as a second language.

English as a Second Language (ESL): ESL is a necessary component of all bilingual education programs. Although the methodologies vary widely, ESL teachers generally focus their instruction on the development of listening, speaking, reading, and writing skills in English by creating low-stress learning environments (i.e., reducing the affective filter) and providing for comprehensible input. The students' vernacular is often used to clarify meaning and enhance understanding. In districts where many language groups are represented or there is a scarcity of bilingual teachers, students may receive ESL instruction only through "pullout classes" a few times a week. According to Ovando, Collier, & Combs (2003), ESL is a system of instruction that enables students who are ELLs to acquire academic proficiency in spoken and written English. The authors also indicate that ESL is an essential component of all bilingual education programs in the United States for students who are ELLs.

Ethnic Group: According to Banks & Banks (2007) an ethnic group may be defined as a microcultural group that shares a common history and culture, values, behaviors, and other characteristics that lead members of the group to have a shared identity. A sense of peoplehood emerges as one of the most important aspects of membership within an ethnic group.

Ethnic Minority Groups: These are groups which tend to be numerical minorities and have distinguishing cultural characteristics, racial characteristics, or both, which makes them easily identifiable and sometimes targeted to other groups (Banks & Banks, 2007).

Ethnocentrism: The belief that one's own culture is not only appropriate for members of that culture but also universally appropriate for every person. Under ethnocentrism the beliefs, cultural practices, values, and traditions of another culture are viewed only through the correctness of one's own cultural lens.

Grammar-Translation Approach: According to Ovando, Collier, & Combs (2003), this approach "usually involves memorizing long vocabulary lists out of context, deductive instruction of grammar in which rules are taught explicitly, practice of extensive verb conjugations that are committed to memory, and reading literature passages through translation, with the teacher serving as an authority figure and providing immediate error correction" (p. 147).

Immersion: The concept of immersion is based on the premise that people learn a second language in the same way they learn their first language—in contexts where they are socially motivated to communicate. Teachers use only the target language. In Canada, English-speaking children with no French language experience entering kindergarten or first grade classes conducted solely in French. Language learning occurs through interaction with meaningful content (California State Department of Education, 1984).

Interdependence Hypothesis: According to Cummins (1981), a student who has mastered the rudiments of reading and thinking in the first language will perform well on entering a second language environment. Common underlying proficiency (CUP) will facilitate a ready transfer of academic skills. Conversely, a child who fails to reach a "threshold level" of development in the mother tongue—for example, an ELL who makes a premature transition to English—is likely to struggle in both languages (Crawford, 1991).

Interference: According to Horwitz (2008), interference "refers to the negative influences or intrusion of the native language on second language learning" (p.244). Interference is also know as negative transfer.

Interlanguage: As defined by Horwitz (2008), interlanguage "refers to the way learners produce the target language. Learners' interlanguages are systematic and reflect their implicit linguistic knowledge" (p. 244). Viewing interlanguage as a creative and rule-governed system, Diaz-Rico (2008) states, "An English language development curriculum that elicits the learner's creativity allows the learner to show the current state of his or her interlanguage. The view that learners have intermediary language modes that are not flawed misrepresentations of English, but rather are natural, creative expressions of the learner's innate language 'genius,' offers a refreshing opportunity for teachers to view second-language learning in a positive light" (p.192.

Language-Minority Students: According to Wong-Fillmore (1991), "language-minority children" refers to children "from homes in which English is not the predominant language of communication between parents and children." Language profiles for these children vary substantially with respect to oral proficiency and literacy in both the home language and in English, and these profiles commonly change on an ongoing basis.

Lau vs. Nichols: According to Ooka Pang (2005), this court ruling was precipitated by a group of Cantonese-speaking parents who " filed a class action suit against the San Francisco School District on behalf of Chinese-speaking children. Lau is Kinney Lau, who was a first grader. Alan Nichols was the superintendent. The Supreme Court ruled in 1974 that students who spoke a language other than English were denied an equal education. This decision led to the inclusion of Bilingual Education programs" (p. G2).

Lexicon: This term can be defined as the set of all the words and idioms of any given language (Richards, Platt, & Platt, 1992).

Linguicism: The practice of discriminating against a person solely because of the language he or she speaks.

Linguistics: The study of human language which, in spite of a long history of development as a science, has only recently been viewed as an independent discipline. It includes a wide field of specializations and different approaches to research. For example, sound systems or phonology, sentence structure or syntax, and meaning systems or semantics and pragmatics (Richards, Platt, & Platt, 1992).

Melting Pot: This is an assimilationist point-of-view. Whether one does this by choice, or one is compelled to by the dominant group, it is a one-way process of giving up one's identity to adopt a new one (Scott, 1992).

Monitor Hypothesis: According to a second language acquisition theory, the monitor functions as an internal "editor." The monitor scans and sorts the rules. A goal of the "Natural Approach" is to reduce the use of the monitor, i.e., avoid speech hesitation or pauses for the purpose of self-correction of errors in language (Krashen, 1982).

Natural Approach: Based on the work of Terrell (1977), this approach includes instructional techniques that facilitate the natural acquisition of language. This approach, which encourages language acquisition by developing proficiency without direct or conscious recourse to the formal rules of the language, is based on two principles: (1) Speech is not taught directly but rather acquired by understanding what is being communicated in low-anxiety environments; and (2) Speech emerges in natural stages, namely, preproduction, early production, speech emergence, intermediate fluency. The focus is on meaning rather than on correctness of form. An initial silent period is a prerequisite to actual speech production by students.

Newcomer Center: This typically refers to a centralized location set up in a school district to process incoming minority (typically recent immigrant) language students. The students undergo screening in a variety of areas, including language assessment in both English and the native language. Orientation classes are conducted to give the students information related to their new school setting, such as health and nutrition and appropriate school behavior. Some newcomer centers are designed to offer intensive English language development lessons which provide students with the communication skills necessary to initially function in the actual school setting. Freinlander (1991) describes a newcomer class as a "temporary transitional program designed to meet the unique needs of newcomer students in the context of a nurturing and supportive educational environment."

INTERCULTURAL UNDERSTANDING

Prejudice: A preconceived attitude, feeling or inclination that is usually based on stereotypical information and directed toward a member of a particular group. As Allport stated in 1954, "A feeling, favorable or unfavorable, toward a person or thing, prior to, or not based on, actual experience" (as quoted in Pang, 2005, p. G-3).

Psycholinguistics: The study of both the mental processes a human utilizes in producing and comprehending language and the manner in which a person may learn language. Psycholinguistics includes multiple aspects including speech perception, the role of memory and concepts and various processes in language use as well as how social and psychological influences may affect the use of language (Richards, Platt, & Platt, 1992).

Semilingualism: A controversial notion that posits that there are some people who have learned two or more languages during different periods in their lives but have not developed a native speaker level of proficiency in any of them (Richards, Platt, & Platt, 1992).

Sheltered English: Sheltered English is used to make academic instruction in English understandable to ELLs. Mainstream subject content is taught using English as the medium of communication to ELLs homogeneously grouped for level of English language proficiency. Emphasis is on vocabulary and concepts, not grammar. This program is modeled after the highly successful French immersion program developed for English-speaking Canadian students.

Sociolinguistics: This is the study of language as a social and cultural phenomenon. Studies of language variation, language and social interaction, and language attitudes are major divisions within the field of sociolinguistics (Center for Applied Linguistics, 1986).

Speech Emergence: This occurs when a child begins to speak. Speech emerges naturally on its own when enough comprehensible input is internalized (Terrell, 1977).

Stereotype: According to Pang (2005), a stereotype is an "overgeneralized image of a person: an untrue fixed picture that has a value judgment attached to it" (p. G-3).

Submersion: Submersion, as distinguished from immersion, is when ELLs receive no services through bilingual or ESL education programs. The submersion approach is also referred to as the "sink or swim" approach in educating ELLs.

Subtractive Bilingual Programs: Also referred to as early exit bilingual programs, these programs generally exit ELLs before the third grade. The goal of these programs is to replace the home language with the second language (English). In such programs original proficiency in the home language is usually lost, hence the term "subtractive." There tends to be much less time for concept development which later impacts student performance as these students encounter a more rigorous curriculum in the upper grades.

Suggestopedy, Suggestopedia, or Suggestology: A method of foreign language teaching developed by Bulgarian psychologist Georgi Lozanov. Through the use of dialogues, situations and translations, students present and practice language. Nonverbal techniques including classical music, visual images, and relaxation exercises are utilized to make learning more comfortable and effective in aesthetic surroundings (Richards, Platt, & Platt, 1992). Lozanov's method advocates the use of a relaxed environment coupled with large amounts of direct teacher input to stimulate alpha brainwaves which lead to super learning (Brown, 2001).

Syntax: According to Richards, Platt, & Platt (1992), syntax is "the study of how words combine to form sentences and the rules which govern the formation of sentences" (p. 370). Pang (2005) explains that even very young toddlers learn how to generate a complete sentence and express a thought or idea. As an example she wrote, "a child may say 'Ann and I is going to school tomorrow.' She knows to place the subject first and then the verb in her sentence so that the word order is correct; however, the child needs to learn about the grammatical rules regarding the use of a verb that denotes a plural subject" (p. 294).

Threshold Hypothesis: Originally stipulated by Cummins in 1979, Richards, Platt, and Platt (1992) define this hypothesis regarding learning a second language as "a certain minimum 'threshold' level of proficiency that must be reached in that language before the learner can benefit from the use of the language as a medium of instruction in school. This hypothesis is related by Cummins to the developmental interdependence hypothesis which says that the development of proficiency in a second language depends upon the level of proficiency the child learner has reached in the first language at the time when extensive exposure to the second language begins" (p. 380).

Total Physical Response (TPR): TPR was developed by psychologist James Asher (1982) as a method for second language teaching that parallels first language acquisition sequences. This approach is based on three key ideas: (1) understanding the spoken language precedes speaking; (2) understanding is developed through students' body movements; and (3) speech should not be forced as students naturally reach a "readiness" point when speech becomes spontaneous. During instruction, commands are given in L2 and acted out first by the teacher then by the students, allowing them to perceive the meaning of the commands while hearing the language. Students begin speaking when they are ready (i.e., there is allowance for a "silent period") and communication is not interrupted by corrections.

Transitional Bilingual Education (TBE): In TBE programs, ELLs study English in classes especially designed for second-language learners and receive a portion of their instruction in their native language to help them keep up in school subjects. The goal of this model is to facilitate the transition of such students into the all-English curriculum by providing native language instructional support as well as English language development. This is the most common type of bilingual education programs in the United States.

Two-Way Bilingual Education: Two-way Bilingual programs are designed to encourage students to learn in two languages and to develop proficiency in both L1 and L2. Two-way or dual-language bilingual programs resemble immersion programs but differ in two respects: (1) the classes have a mixed enrollment of ELLs and native English-speaking students, and (2) the ELLs generally receive some English language instruction from the outset. The goal is to produce bilingualism in the entire group of participants, regardless of the students' language background.

References

Asher, J (1982). *Learning another language through actions: The complete teacher's guidebook.* Los Gatos, CA: Sky Oaks Publications.
Banks, J. A. & Banks, C.A.M. (2007). *Multicultural education: Issues and perspectives.* Hoboken, NJ: John Wiley and Sons, Inc.
Banks, J.A. (1986). *Teaching ethnic studies: Concepts and strategies* (4th ed.). Boston: Allyn and Bacon.
Brown, H.D. (1994). *Principles of language learning and teaching.* Englewood Cliffs, NJ: Prentice Hall Regents.
Brown, H. D. (2001). *Teaching by principles: An interactive approach to language pedagogy.* White plains, NY: Addison Wesley Longman, Inc.
California State Department of Education. (1984) *Studies on immersion education.* Sacramento, CA: Author.

Center for Applied Linguistics. (1986 December). *What is linguistics?* Washington, DC: Center for Applied Linguistics Clearinghouse on Languages and Linguistics.

Chamot, A. & O'Malley, J.M. (1987, June). The cognitive academic language learning approach: A bridge to the mainstream. *TESOL Quarterly, 21* (2), 227-235.

Cortés, C. (1993, March). Acculturation, assimilation, and "adducation." *BE Outreach.* Sacramento, CA: Bilingual Education Office, California State Department of Education.

Crawford, J. (1991). *Bilingual education: History, politics, theory and practice.* Los Angeles, CA: Bilingual Educational Services.

Cummins, J. (1981). *The role of primary language development in promoting educational success for language minority students.* Sacramento: California State Department of Education, Office of Bilingual Bicultural Education.

Diaz-Rico, L.T. (2008). *A course for teaching English learners.* Boston: Pearson Education, Inc.

Fillmore, L.W., & Snow, C.E. (2000). *What teachers need to know about language.* Washington, DC: US Department of Education.

Freeman, Y., Freeman, D., & Mercuri, S. P.(2005). *Dual language essentials.* Portsmouth, NH: Heinemann.

Freindlander, M. (1991). *The newcomer program: Helping immigrant students succeed in U.S. in U.S. schools.* Washington, DC: National Clearinghouse for Bilingual Education.

Gay, G. (2000). *Culturally responsive teaching: Theory, research, and practice.* New York: Teachers College Press.

Gollnick, D. M., & Chinn, P.C. (2006). *Multicultural education in a pluralistic society.* Upper Saddle River, NJ: Pearson Prentice Hall.

Horwitz, E.K. (2008). *Becoming a language teacher.* Boston: Pearson Education, Inc.

Jacobson, R. (1981). The implementation of a bilingual instruction model: The new concurrent approach. In R. V. Padilla (Ed.),

Ethnoperspectives in bilingual education research, Vol. 3: Bilingual education technology (pp. 14-29). Ypsilanti, MI: Eastern Michigan University.

Krashen, S.D. (1982). *Principles and practice in second language acquisition.* New York: Pergamon Press.

Krashen, S.D. (1985). *The input hypothesis: Issues and implications.* New York: Longman.

Nieto, S., & Bode, P. (2008). *Affirming diversity: The sociopolitical context of multicultural education.* Boston: Pearson Education, Inc.

Ovando, C. J., Collier, V.P., & Combs, M.C. (2003). *Bilingual and ESL classrooms.* New York: McGraw-Hill Book Company.

Pang, V. O. (2005). *Multicultural education: A caring-centered, reflective approach.* NY: The McGraw-Hill Companies, Inc.

Richards, J.C., Platt, J., & Platt, H. (1992). *Longman dictionary of language teaching & applied linguistics.* Essex, England: Longman Group UK Limited.

Scott, B. (1992). *Multicultural education: An overview for practitioners.* San Antonio, TX: Intercultural Development Research Association.

Terrell, T. (1977). A natural approach to second language acquisition and learning. *Modern Language Journal, 61,* 325-337.

Wong-Fillmore, L. (1991). Language and cultural issues in the early education of language-minority children. In S. Kagan (Ed.), *The care and education of American's young children: Obstacles and opportunities.* Ninetieth Yearbook of the National Society for the Study of Education, Part I (pp. 30-49). Chicago: University of Chicago Press.

Call for Manuscripts

During the latter part of the 20th century the call for reform in teacher education was based partially on the need to reduce the negative impact of the mismatch of a rapidly increasing diverse student population and a teaching force that was largely not diverse. Substantially more than 5 million English language learners are enrolled in U.S. public schools while the number of new teachers who are adequately prepared to effectively teach newcomers who are learning English lags far behind the need. As the culturally and linguistically diverse segment of the school population in the United States continues to rapidly grow in the 21st century, it is imperative that preservice and inservice teachers possess the skills, attitudes, knowledge base, and intercultural understanding necessary for facilitating success for all students.

Upon entering U.S. schools linguistically diverse students encounter unique challenges including the need to learn the English language simultaneously with content area information. They also have considerable needs as do their culturally diverse counterparts. These needs include the invitation to participate, acceptance by teachers and other students, and seeing not only themselves, but also their experiences reflected in the school curriculum. The expectation of most students and their parents including those who are linguistically and ethnically diverse is that their teachers will understand how to lead them academically through equitable and effective instructional practice while at the same time attending to their affective development in understanding of self and others. Meeting such an expectation requires that teachers have extensive knowledge of students, parents, cultures, languages, as well as appropriate programs and materials.

Additionally, embedded in the current debate regarding immigration reform is the national policy for language and language difference. The purpose for bilingual education and English as a second language programs, which is to facilitate fluency and literacy in English for English language learners (ELLs), continues to be misunderstood and at times seems to be lost in the debate. What aspects of bilingual and ESL education should be clarified so that the general public has a clearer understanding of the goals and objectives of such programs? What are the components of a quality bilingual program? What strategies are most effective in teaching English as a second language? What factors must be considered when designing exemplary programs and instruction for ELLs?

In order to further the dialogue regarding bilingual and ESL education in the United States, the Bilingual/ESL Committee of the Federation of North Texas Area Universities proposes to prepare a monograph entitled **Current Issues and Best Practices in Bilingual and ESL Education**. Third in a series of monographs addressing critical issues in the education of English language learners, the monograph will be a compendium of information, current trends, and research associated with exploring significant themes and exceptional practice in the field of bilingual and ESL education. Interested authors are invited to submit scholarly papers on topics related to current issues and best practices in bilingual and ESL education. Suggested topics include dual language programs, the effective use of teacher assistants, working with and involving diverse parents and communities, immigration reform issues, reading and writing in the content areas, bilingual literacy, sheltering instruction, formal and informal assessment concerns, culturally relevant and culturally responsive teaching, administering diverse populations, error analysis and comparative analysis of English and other languages, multicultural education and the English language learner, cross-cultural communication, ESL and content area instruction, language policy in the United States, successful bilingual and ESL programs, book reviews, and ESL and the newcomer. For more information you may contact Dr. Melinda Cowart, Managing Editor, at mcowart@mail.twu.edu or Dr. Phap Dam, Series Editor, at pdam@mail.twu.edu. The anticipated audience for the monograph will be preservice and inservice teachers and administrators in addition to university faculty and students. The deadline for submission is November 1, 2007. Guidelines for authors follow.

Guidelines for Authors

Manuscripts must adhere to the following guidelines:

1. Length: The manuscript, including references, charts and tables should not exceed 20 typewritten pages.
2. Type: The document should be completed in Microsoft Word. The font should be 12 point and in Times New Roman.
3. Style: Manuscripts must conform to the Publication Manual of the American Psychological Association (APA), 5th edition (2001).
4. Cover letter: Include a cover letter explaining the relationship of your scholarly paper to the theme of the monograph. Provide a statement indicating that the paper is original material and is not under consideration for publication elsewhere.
5. Title Page: Include the following information on a separate page:
    Title of manuscript
    Author's name
    Complete mailing address
    E-mail address
    Business and home phone numbers
    Institutional affiliation and address
    Biographical data about each author
6. Abstract: Submit an abstract of 100-150 words.

7. Miscellaneous: Spelling, grammar, and accuracy of references are the responsibility of the authors.
8. Copies: Submit two double-spaced paper copies of the manuscript along with an e-mail attachment to Dr. Melinda Cowart, Managing Editor, (mcowart@mail.twu.edu). Her mailing address is: Dr. Melinda Cowart, Department of Teacher Education, Texas Woman's University, P. O. Box 425769, Denton, TX 76204-5769. Copies submitted for consideration for publication will not be returned. Deadline: November 1, 2007
9. Book Reviews: Book reviews should be in APA format and no longer than 5 pages.

Authors' Information

Dr. Phap Dam, a native of Vietnam, is professor and coordinator of the Bilingual and ESL Education Program in the Department of Teacher Education at Texas Woman's University. His areas of expertise include second-language acquisition theories and practices, multicultural education, and comparative linguistics. He has published monographs and articles in language education, translated Spanish poetry into Vietnamese, and spoken at state, national, and international conferences on language education. Dr. Dam is the series editor for the current series of monographs on issues affecting English language learners and their teachers.

Dr. Melinda Cowart began her career in bilingual education in 1975. She has been a bilingual educator in elementary school, an ESL teacher in middle school and is currently an associate professor of teacher education in the bilingual program at Texas Woman's University. She and her husband, Mr. Ron Cowart, have worked extensively with refugee youth and adults. Her research interests include the effective, equitable education for linguistically and ethnically diverse students and the appropriate preparation of teachers who will be teaching diverse populations. Dr. Cowart is managing editor for the current series of monographs on issues affecting English language learners and their teachers.

Dr. Gina Anderson is an assistant professor in the Department of Teacher Education at Texas Woman's University. She teaches curriculum and educational foundations courses in the Professional Studies program. Her research areas include multicultural/diversity issues, middle level education, and professional pre-service and in-service teacher development.

Dr. Elizabeth Carver-Cyr is an adjunct professor in the School of Educational Studies at Oklahoma State University. She teaches educational foundations and social studies methods courses. She is also a middle school classroom practitioner. Her research areas include multicultural issues and the professional growth of teachers.

Dr. Emily Chou is an assistant professor of English at Chihlee Institute of Technology in Taiwan. She holds a Ph. D. in reading education from Texas Woman's University. Her research interests include Chinese-English contrastive analysis, learning strategies, bilingual literacy, and factors that affect the acquisition of English by international students in the United States.

Dr. Lloyd Kinnison is a professor of special education at Texas Woman's University. He is the coordinator of the doctoral program and educational diagnostician preparation. His research interests include the application of CALP to special populations, response to instruction, assessment issues and students will intellectual disabilities.

Dr. Tammy L. Stephens is an assistant professor of special education at the University of Texas at Tyler. A formal special education teacher and educational diagnostician, her research interests include the identification of appropriate assessment techniques, which include curriculum-based measurement, early intervention practices, and the identification of appropriate instructional strategies for diverse learners.

Mr. Phillip Stager is a Spanish teacher at Plano West Senior High School and is currently pursuing his doctorate in Special Education at Texas Woman's University. He is a graduate of Texas Tech University and earned his Master's degree at Southern Methodist University in bilingual education. His research interests include the development and implementation of instructional strategies for diverse learners in foreign language settings and Spanish literacy development.

INTERCULTURAL UNDERSTANDING

Ms. Jessica A. Rueter is a practicing secondary diagnostician for Northwest Independent School District in Justin, Texas. Jessica is pursuing a doctoral degree at Texas Woman's University in special education. She is currently finishing class work requirements and is in the data analysis phase of a pilot study for her dissertation.

Dr. Janelle Mathis, an associate professor, teaches graduate and undergraduate courses in literacy instruction for diverse classrooms and children's literature at the University of North Texas. Her research interests include the selection and use of children's literature about issues of identity, diversity, social justice, and the global society.

Dr. Joyce Ann Rademacher is a professor of special education at Texas Woman's University. She prepares teachers to teach students with mild/moderate disabilities. Her research interests include the development and validation of strategic interventions for diverse learners in inclusive settings.

Dr. Karen Dunlap, an assistant professor in the Department of Teacher Education at Texas Woman's University, currently teaches undergraduate educational foundations courses. Her areas of interest include identity formation, reflective thinking, student voice, and teacher preparation.

Dr. Jane B. Pemberton is an associate professor in the Special Education Program, Department of Teacher Education, College of Professional Education, Texas Woman's University. Her research interests include instructional strategies for all learners, inclusive practices, and curriculum-based assessment.

Dr. Ron W. Wilhelm is a professor in the department of teacher education and administration at the University of North Texas. He serves as director of the Center for the Study of Education Reform. His current research focus is the educational challenges of Spanish speaking immigrants.

INTERCULTURAL UNDERSTANDING

Dr. Judi Repman is a professor of instructional technology and Director of the Center for International Schooling at Georgia Southern University, Statesboro, GA. Her B.A., M.L.S., and Ph.D. are from Louisiana State University, Baton Rouge. She is interested in all aspects of international schooling and school reform and is particularly interested in how technology can be used to facilitate intercultural understanding.

Dr. Cindi Chance is the Dean of the College of Education at Georgia Southern University. She has been involved in intercultural research and practice ranging from inner city, to rural to international. Her professional research and practice has involved teaching from kindergarten to doctoral levels in multiple states.

Dr. Stephanie Kenney is Associate Dean of the College of Education at the University of Southern Georgia. She has worked in collaboration with colleagues and other universities to develop foreign study opportunities through the USG Center for International Schooling.

Dr. Pat Parsons is Director of Field Experiences and Partnerships within the College of Education at the University of Southern Georgia. Dr. Parsons has worked in collaboration with the Center for International Schooling to develop opportunities for student teaching in foreign countries.

Dr. Pat Henderson Casey is an assistant professor at Texas Woman's University. Dr. Casey joined TWU after serving the Texas public schools as a bilingual elementary school teacher, an assistant principal and principal. Her research interests include preparation of teachers and school leaders for diverse populations and, especially, bilingual education.

INTERCULTURAL UNDERSTANDING

Dr. Michelle Abrego is an assistant professor in the Educational Leadership Program at the University of Texas at Brownsville. Her research interests include family involvement, teacher induction, as well as teacher and principal preparation programs. Her background experience in education includes that of serving as a teacher, principal and program coordination at state education agency.

Dr. Patsy J. Robles-Goodwin is an assistant professor in Early Childhood Education at the University of North Texas. She is a former elementary bilingual/ESL teacher and school administrator. Her research interests include educational issues affecting Latino families and students, young children and linguistic/literacy issues, and diversity teaching and training.

Dr. Dora Salazar is a member of the bilingual teacher education faculty at Texas Tech University. Her research interests include bilingual and ESL education and strategies for working effectively with the parents of diverse student populations.

Dr. Mary F. B. Garza is director of the bilingual program at Midwestern State University. A classroom teacher for 13 years, Dr. Garza has also worked in the Texas Education Agency with both the Division of Migrant Education and the Bilingual Education Program. Her research interests include the use of music and writing with language development in the bilingual classroom, distance learning with migrant and bilingual early education, parental involvement, and teacher preparation.

Dr. Rudy Rodriguez, visiting professor of Bilingual/ESL Teacher Education at the University of North Texas, was a teacher in secondary education prior to becoming the first director of the bilingual/ESL education program in the Fort Worth Independent School District. In 2002, Dr. Rodriguez transferred to the University of North Texas after 27 years as a bilingual/ESL teacher educator at Texas Woman's University.